AFTER THE WEDDING

DAVID THORNTON-WAKEFORD

AFTER THE WEDDING

AN ALBATROSS BOOK

Published in Australia and New Zealand by
Albatross Books Pty Ltd
PO Box 320, Sutherland
NSW 2232, Australia
in the United States of America by
Albatross Books Pty Ltd
PO Box 131, Claremont
CA 91711, USA
and in the United Kingdom by
Lion Publishing plc
Peter's Way, Sandy Lane West
Oxford OX4 5HG, England

First edition 1996

National Library of Australia
Cataloguing-in-Publication data

Thornton-Wakeford, David
After the Wedding: creating a stable, secure marriage

ISBN 0 7324 1030 4

1. Marriage. I. Thornton-Wakeford, David. II. Title.

306.81

Cover photograph: Graham Horner
Printed and bound in Australia by Griffin Paperbacks, Netley, SA

Contents

This book is dedicated to Jack Dominian,
who first used the phrase, and
in thanksgiving for my parents,
William and Rosalie, who gave me:
'THE BLISSFUL CERTAINTY OF BEING WANTED'

Acknowledgments

My wife, Deborah, and my three children originally gave me the space to write this book during four weeks in 1992 when I had some study leave. It took another eighteen months to find the time to get it into final draft formation for publishing and they endured my consequent frustration due to some sickness and pressure of work. May God bless them out of their socks!

Thanks be to both the Anglican Parish of Applecross and to Archbishop Peter Carnley of Perth, for financing the study leave.

I thank a very special lady, Julie Biggs, who provided me with my spiritual retreat, a little room overlooking the Swan River at Applecross, where I could write in quietness, gazing often at the tranquil view. And when I got stuck, I would go for a stroll along the foreshore. Wonderful!

A huge debt of gratitude is due to Daphne Pyke who has so tirelessly and painstakingly worked away on her computer at the manuscript. I am also grateful for her advice on a number of finer points and for the editing she has done.

Kinway Anglican Marriage and Family Counselling Services in Perth and Canon Greg Harvey helped with resources in Appendix A and Appendix C.

I am grateful to the people whose names and situations

have been changed to protect their anonymity and whose stories are told in this book.

Thanks be to God.

Unless otherwise indicated, all scriptural quotations are from the New Revised Standard Version of the Bible, The National Council of Churches, USA, 1990, used with permission.

Occasional references are made to my first book, *If Fish Is All You Want*, Anglican Design Display and Print, Perth, 1983.

Introduction

MARRIAGE IS STILL THE MOST POPULAR WAY TO GO in a relationship; eighty per cent of young Australians choose this course of action. There is a lot of glamour attached to a wedding and to the process of getting to the big day.

But what happens then? Is there life after the wedding? It seems that once you arrive at your wedding *day* there are very few support systems out there for the actual *marriage*. The sanctity of marriage and the family needs emphasising more today than ever before, for the stability and integrity of family life is threatened on every side. Nearly forty per cent of first marriages are ending in divorce; nearly fifty per cent of second marriages go the same way.

The average reader will already be more than aware of numbers of relationships that are experiencing difficulties. The writer doesn't know anyone over the age of twenty-five who hasn't experienced or discovered relationship breakdown in his or her immediate circle of family and friends. The good news is that many relationships are flourishing — they are very stable and highly satisfying.

Why is this breakdown in marriages taking place? There are some subtle changes in our society that have brought this about. One of these is people's longevity. Archbishop Robert Runcie, the former Archbishop of Canterbury, stated in 1984:

> *One of the reasons why failure in marriage is a particular problem today is its length. Two hundred years ago, the average marriage would have lasted fifteen years; now it's more like fifty. It's a lot to ask young people to be faithful for that length of time, especially when by faithful we mean not just docile, well-behaved, but romantic and companionable.*[1]

There is no doubt that society today has conditioned us to expect more of marriage than former generations have. In his book *Make or Break*, Jack Dominian says:

> *The ideal of contemporary marriage is indeed lofty. Its consummation needs an equivalent degree of insight and perseverance. . . The personal and sexual world of contemporary marriage has been shaped by a variety of social and psychological factors which collectively have raised the level of awareness of the meaning of love in marriage.*[2]

There is a long list of modern-day influences working against good marriages — the role changes in the family brought about by economic influences have significantly affected good communication between partners; many old values and standards have been eroded or destroyed; divorce is easier and less controversial; there is a cultural environment geared more and more to the self, often supported by a popular media which only encourages romantic love rather than the deeper love of personal commitment.

People are more isolated and have less self-esteem; financial stress, particularly in one-income families, is exacerbated by lengthy recession and the fear of unemployment; and greater financial independence brought about through a higher proportion of earning couples makes separation easier — these are some of many such influences.

A particularly destructive trend which is gaining momentum in the minds of people is the presupposition that, if there is something wrong with your relationship, then you are 'incompatible' and it can't work. There is less room for negotiation in a society influenced by the 'instant' (coffee, credit. . .) and the 'disposable' (cameras, nappies. . .). We know that if a product doesn't work to our complete satisfaction, we can put it aside for another one. Why should our relationships be any different?

Changes like these have meant that many people today are bewildered and discouraged about marriage (and indeed, about life in general). Children and adolescents often become cynical to protect themselves from the pain of seeing their parents' or friends' parents' relationships breakdown. Yet the need for mutual nurturing, protection, intimacy, companionship and growth, which is the substance of a satisfactory, stable marriage, still remains paramount. And it is this sort of marriage that I believe the wedding should be about.

While this book is a look at some causes and symptoms of marriage breakdown, it is mostly about exploring some foundations to stable relationships. It takes a close look at the many faceted diamond of love, which provides the solid rock to which we can anchor, a rock that stands the test of time.

I believe there *is* life after the wedding — a full and rich life. Each day we are given a fresh invitation to fall in love, for we were created for love, in love, to love. We simply need to take the time to seek and find it.

Part A:
Marriages built on shaky ground

I will not live for pleasure! I will not live for power!
I will not surrender responsibility for my life
and my actions.

John Powell

1

Society's unstated 'rules'

GRAHAM AND JENNY, LIKE MANY COUPLES today, had been living together for quite some time before their marriage. They felt it was a good preparation for marriage and their relationship during this time was very strong. For much of this period, Jenny wore an engagement ring. Their friends and relations were thrilled for them and eagerly anticipated the wedding day.

The quality of Graham and Jenny's courtship was particularly evident to anyone who met them. They were so in love. Like most couples today, they were both income earners and the time they made for each other after work and on weekends was paramount in their thinking. Furthermore, they were 'allowed' this time by their work-mates, friends and acquaintances. There didn't seem to be any pressure on them to conform to others' expectations. They had their own individual pastimes as well; it wasn't as if they were all consumed by each other. There seemed to be a good blending of shared interests, togetherness and separate, personal space.

On the day of their wedding, it was plain to see that their relationship was uppermost in their minds — nothing else could have come close — not their work, not their individual interests, not peer pressure, not other people's expectations.

But then something changed. After the magic mountain-top experience of the wedding, reception and honeymoon, within weeks of the rings being placed on their fingers, something changed. Fortunately, Graham and Jenny were more prepared for it than most; they are in the minority of couples prepared for the enormous change that occurs once the wedding ring is upon the finger.

Graham elucidated on just one of these changes shortly after returning from the honeymoon and resuming his office job. After work one day, he joined some of the office staff for drinks at a nearby hotel. The telephone rang and the woman at the bar asked if a 'Graham' was there and if he could speak to his wife.

When Graham returned from his telephone conversation, his workmates stirred him over the fact that his wife had rung him and that he was already 'tied to her apron strings'. He responded, 'My wife is my greatest asset', which is hardly the macho-ocker thing to say, but he said it — and with much pride. Four weeks beforehand, if it had been Jenny his then girlfriend/fiancée, albeit live-in lover, who had telephoned, his companions wouldn't have batted their eyelids.

✠ The unwritten 'rules' that affect marriage

I have known too many couples who have courted well and some who have lived together well, then married disastrously. (Certainly, the statistics do reveal that living together proves very little about marriage anyway, regardless of any stance on its morality, which is not the issue in question here.)

The reason is simple: the rules change and they change for the worse instead of the better. These rules are unwritten, but they are very real and, because they change, often the priorities in a marriage very quickly change as well. Graham and Jenny's priorities on their wedding day, roughly in a descending order, would have been: us, our families and friends, our work, our interests, our leisure time, our individual time.

Ambition and peer pressure can very quickly change this order, along with the assumption-making that creeps in unawares as couples begin to take each other for granted in a more relaxed but lethal 'now we're married, dear' mode. Within often just a few weeks, not even months or years, the order of priority can change to: my individual (or, more accurately, my independent) time, my work and friends, my interests, then my marriage, then our family and friends. In some marriages, almost overnight, the priority of togetherness-time gives way to overtime and peer-influenced social/sport/leisure activity.

Howell Witt puts it delightfully:

> *And there's the bloke who worships his business. He says it's his business — he owns it. And he's the only person in his house who can't see the opposite is the case; the business owns him. Even his eight-year-old son can see it.*[1]

The 'rules' I refer to are, in fact, imposed externally upon us by the society around us. No-one actually taught people these rules; that's what makes them even more sinister. We don't have to keep them, obey them or serve them — but if we do, they will break us and all that is really precious to us in life. They apply both to men and women.

Here are just ten of these rules; there are plenty more:

1. You must earn more money to survive in life and to have a good marriage.
2. You must keep in with your peers — their support and approval is more important than anyone else's (including your spouse's).
3. Enjoy hearing about other people's failings. Whenever possible, be negative.

4. Be open about values and standards. After all, it's a free country.
5. You must maintain your independence even though you're married. Don't be tied down.
6. Do it 'your way' — you don't need anyone else's help. (Frank Sinatra shouldn't take all the credit.)
7. Don't show your feelings. To admit you are wrong is a sign of weakness.
8. Take your partner and your family for granted.
9. Concentrate on your rights and privileges.
10. If ever dissatisfied, try another 'product'.

Many of these rules don't appear in courtship or even when couples are living together because they are often on best behaviour and society encourages them to make their love-nest a real priority. But once some or all of these rules begin to be kept, a disaster is guaranteed sooner or later in marriage or any worthwhile relationship.

✠ The changing face of the society in which these 'rules' operate

Charles Court, former premier of Western Australia, stated in 1991 that society lacked the moral fibre to cope with a depression on the scale of the 1930s. Civil disobedience and anarchy would erupt if the world experienced such a depression again because of the weaker influence of the family, the church and the wider community. The influence of such institutions has deteriorated in tandem with Australia's ethical standards.

Australia's economic woes were as much about this as they were about finance. To many, the difference between right and wrong — ethical and non-ethical conduct — is blurred if not completely ignored. The attitude among many Australians to business fraud was a case of 'if you can get away with something, it's clever — only fools get found out!'[2]

Since then, we have seen former political leaders, even former police commissioners, end up in court and in gaol. This attitude is not just reserved for high-flying business people — it pervades all levels of society.

✠ The 'rules' can be broken

It doesn't have to be this way. All the above 'rules', and more, can be broken and done away with. The truth isn't too hard to find. . .

I had the joy of seeing the delightful American film, *Regarding Henry*, starring Harrison Ford. Some have described it as 'schmaltzy', but its focus is the very temptation just described. It took a couple of bullets, a whole new start to life — learning to walk and talk again — to give the once high-flying, successful lawyer, Henry, the marriage and child he never really had before. It reminded me of the words of Jesus in Mark 8, verse 36: 'For what will it profit them to gain the whole world and forfeit their life?'

Many adult people are caught up with ambition, keeping-up-with-the-Joneses, giving their children a grand education, or saving for that all-significant holiday or dream home — and they don't recognise their most important gift when it stares them in the face at home. We can often just go through the motions of saying 'I love you' as we race out the door, or quickly zoom over the kids' school projects with preoccupied approval. But to *make* that quality time and *be* that available person, to love, to watch, really to listen, feel and yearn — because what is facing us across the kitchen table is our greatest asset — is quite another thing. A sacred thing.

I have a book in my library which is on loan to me — it seems, permanently, because I can't contact the owner who must have moved. Maybe I'm meant to have it! It's called *Inside Out*. I've photocopied one portion of a page which I have stuck in quite a few different places where my eyes frequently rest. The words could easily be my own:

> *I want to do more than exercise kindness toward my wife; I want to freely give to her from deep resources within me. I want to do more than teach my kids what's expected of them and then enforce rules to keep them in line; I want to draw them by my life into the pursuit of God. I want to do more than preach sermons that are biblically sound, well-delivered and warmly received; I want to pour out my soul in ways that convey truth with personal power. I want to do more than control my tendency toward depression; I want to taste the goodness of God to such an extent that I'm confident of perfect joy ahead.*[3]

In my work, I sometimes find myself almost overwhelmed by the needs of so many people. I need space for myself and my family: my greatest assets.

✠ A challenge to the 'rules': independence and individuality are not the same thing

We confuse the definitions of 'individual' and 'independent' at our peril. To be married and independent is a contradiction in terms. Yet how often one hears people say, 'I need my independence, too, you know!' What these people may *really* be saying is, 'I want my individual needs and space affirmed and respected.' The difference between the two is chalk and cheese.

To impose one's own decision upon one's partner or to take some important action without consultation is to act independently. For example, Ann comes home on Friday night and tells John, 'I'm off to golf with the girls tomorrow. We've decided to make it a regular Saturday morning outing.' John reacts, 'Don't I get a say in this, then?' Ann assumed that because she wanted to play golf, John would be happy with the decision she had made independently of him.

The scenario could be quite different, but with the same desired result for Ann. 'John, some of the girls and I thought a regular round of golf on Saturday mornings would be good fun. Is that okay with you?'

To be married *is* to depend. When we say our wedding vows to each other, that is what we mean. 'From now on I am not complete without you.' Our husband or wife should be the most dependable person we know. But often this is not the case. I hear statements from married people all the time that hint of independence and a breakdown in communication. 'I never know where he is after work'... 'She's forever blowing the credit card limit'. . . 'He's more into his football mates than spending time with me'... 'She never wants to know how my day's been.'

How quickly 'my wife' becomes 'the wife' or 'the missus' in pub circles. This is another, perhaps unconscious act of macho independence while one engages in the serious business of drinking with one's mates, knowing full well that dinner was negotiated an hour ago.

A simple arrangement can break the 'don't be tied down' rule without either partner feeling tied down. Each morning, when you go your separate ways, always have a rough idea when you'll be connecting in the evening — the children, too. When that time comes, try the 'half-hour rule'. (This one is a *good* rule!) When about half an hour elapses from the time you planned to be home, get on the phone and make contact. Even if the whole night is changed, the contact has been made. This is just another way of saying, 'I love you, I care about us as a dependent whole.' There's nothing 'tied down' — indeed, the opposite is the case; this action is liberating. You know where you stand. You can relax and get on with things, knowing that your partner (or child) is okay and is thinking about you. (Although beware if it happens too often!)

In marriage, we are meant to be 'partners who complete each other's being'.[4] A marriage is a unity of two people who are no longer themselves without the other — but neither does this mean that their separate personalities are swamped by each other. Rather it means a blending — a moving inwards — like two hands joined, meshing finger to finger. I am meant to be more fully myself because of my lover's presence in my life. The poet Edwin Muir described a healthy bonding as one where '*each asks of each what each most wants to give and each awakes in each what else would never be*'.[5] This is the stuff of true marriage!

Is it any wonder that some people who have been married for a long time begin to think each other's thoughts, feel each other's feelings, see through each other's eyes and dream each other's dreams? And is it any wonder that when, in such marriage, a partner dies that the other feels cut in half? If you have a partner, think about the ways she or he awakes in you 'what else would never be'.

Pause for a moment and celebrate.

If modern Australian men could know the compassion and freedom of Christ, history would be changed.

John Smith

2

Pride

PRIDE IS THE MASTER KEY of all that distorts our true purpose in this life and it is the key to the breakdown of most marriages.

The expression 'pride goes before a fall' comes straight out of the Bible (in Proverbs 16, verse 18). Most of us know the feeling — of going like a bull at a gate with our own plans and then falling flat on our faces. Pride is haughty, undue self-value — out of all proportion to our actual status in God's plan. We are made in God's image, according to Genesis 1, to glorify our creator; we cannot do that if we are so busy glorifying ourselves.

I saw a marvellous card in a newsagency which read: 'You're the most wonderful person in the world and that's not just my opinion. . . [turn over]. . . it's yours!'

Pride has many guises. Some take pride in their looks, others in their race, some in their business, others in their social life or possessions. Pride may be spiritual, intellectual, material or social. Pride can quickly undermine a relationship.

✠ Pride in the guise of familiarity

They say that familiarity breeds contempt. This happens in many marriages, often quite soon after the wedding. Jesus said something similar when he observed, in Luke 4:

'. . .no prophet is accepted in the prophet's hometown'. Why is it that we frequently fail really to hear, and to respond to, those who are close to us? It is in our closest relationships that pride can often reap the most destruction.

When did we last cherish a piece of advice, a word of gentle, loving rebuke, a simple but prophetic insight, *because* it came from someone close? Here lies the miracle and joy of true love, yet often shied away from because of pride and spiritual blindness. Pride so cleverly and so frequently kills all that is good in human relationships and in our relationship with God as well. We tend to love digging in our heels — we will not give in! We refuse to budge an inch even while we notice the bad taste it is leaving in our mouths.

I have seen marriages, families, office staff, church groups destroyed because of this. It is usually because people can't look past their own noses — or they will not. When I see this happen among Christians, I find it doubly alarming. Where is Christ when these things happen? — the one who constantly thought and acted in relation to others, the one who washed dirty feet, the one who approached a man who had even disowned him and asked him, 'Do you love me?'

No, Jesus wouldn't sit there in his corner either navel-gazing or feeling sorry for himself, not even on the cross.

✠ Pride in the guise of anger and resentment

Anger and resentment are always close by in these things. Many of us know only too well what it is like to be first the victim and then the attacker in the pecking order of anger. I have worked with enough broken marriages now to discover a consistent pattern of bondage and destruction.

The scenarios may vary, but the result is the same: Johnny has a tantrum because he can't find his toy. Mum tells him to look properly and raises her voice to screaming pitch. Dad tells her not to yell at the lad, she's always doing it, and he loses his cool. Mum snaps back, saying that if he got home a bit earlier each night and helped her with the children, it would be a lot better.

He comes right back with the financial position that he's trying hard to improve. . . doesn't she care about their standard of living? They now quarrel. The anger increases. The children retreat, not enjoying their parents like this. The couple argues all the way to bed. Eventually, the lights go out and there is silence. The problem is still not settled. They 'get physical'.

The next morning, things are worse. They stare daggers at each other over the cornflakes. This is because they have confused anger and love. They have not reconstructed their love in order to 'make love'. One has simply used the other for momentary satisfaction and, in so doing, has cheapened an intimate gift. Resentment and bitterness then arrive and the last state of that episode is worse than the first.

Paul speaks words of wisdom in his Letter to the Ephesians: 'Be angry but do no sin; do not let the sun go down on your anger.' It is not too hard to see what this means in terms that are quite familiar for most of us. Richard Holloway observes that this can be the phase of 'slow death', leading to total breakdown:

> *Members of the same family can cease to address a single word to each other; husband and wife can live under the same roof and never exchange a meaningful remark; members of the same congregation can snub each other for years, living out a hideous contradiction of the faith they profess, for a reason they have long since forgotten.*

This is anger at its final and most malignant phase.[1]

When it comes to actual separation and divorce, the bitterness can increase further so that the last state of the unhappy proceedings is again far worse than the first: these devouring monsters that were once so deeply devoted to each other!

In my experience, if they still had the objectivity left to look back at the time they *thought* they had insurmountable problems, many couples would see them as chicken-feed compared to the diabolical mess they have allowed to destroy totally any chances of reconciliation. And sadly, the statistics do reveal that the grass is rarely greener on the other side of a first marriage because we take most of the original problems with us unless we are prepared to deal with them beforehand.

I have felt like saying to individuals sometimes, 'If you really want to know what's wrong with your marriage, go and look in a mirror.' We are often so quick to project our issues onto others.

Frances de Sales, Bishop of Geneva in the early seventeenth century, said on a related matter:

> *. . .though reason requires that when we are at fault, we should be displeased and sorry, yet we must prevent ourselves from having a displeasure which is bitter, sulky, spiteful and angry. Many people commit a great fault because, when they have given way to anger, they are annoyed for being annoyed and angry at having been angry and upset; for this is the way they keep their hearts preserved and steeped in anger.*[2]

We can understand why Jesus says in Matthew 5: 'You have heard that it was said to those of ancient times, you shall not murder; and whoever murders shall be liable to judgment. But I say to you that if you are angry with a brother or sister, you will be liable to judgment; and if you insult a brother or sister, you will be liable to the council; and if you say, "You fool", you will be liable to the hell of fire.' Jesus could see what anger, unchecked, could lead to.

It is not a sin simply to feel anger, especially if it is righteous anger; it is not a sin to deal *creatively* with anger; it *is* a sin to let anger give way, through pride and false judgment, to bitterness, shame, jealousy and a multitude of harmful things that do bind us into our own private hell.

Anger not only brings out our cruellest nature; it hinders Christian witness. Look at Northern Ireland, the Holy Land, Bosnia.

On a more domestic level, I know a woman who was very anxious for her husband to find a relationship with Christ. One day, in talking with him, he disclosed to me that his wife had a temper that would flare up at the drop of a hat. This was a blockage for him, and understandably so. We read in Galatians 5 that two 'works of the flesh' are enmity and strife; they are opposed to the 'fruit of the Spirit' — the same fruit which this woman obviously desired for her husband as a consequence of his hopeful conversion.

Later, she and I prayed together about this stumbling block and especially for a genuine demonstration of 'love, joy, peace, patience, kindness, generosity, faithfulness, gentleness and self-control'. As she began to control her temper, so her husband slowly began to reassess her faith in Christ. It became more authentic for him.

However, this leads us to another serious aspect in the scheme of pride.

✠ Pride in the guise of 'macho' behaviour

'Macho' pride is a particularly sinister strain. It not only often rebels from a good dependent relationship in marriage; it also rebels from a relationship with God. The one who seriously believes that 'I did it my way' is the motto of life will never experience any depth in a relationship — indeed, will often see a union disintegrate for lack of nurture or desire for growth. This syndrome affects men more than women. The Protestant work ethic has distorted many men's awareness of their innermost need to depend and to know that it is all right to ask for help.

Consequently, men are more isolationist than women. Men don't need a 'crutch', some will say; that is why you won't see as many men in churches as women. It can even go deeper; some men are jealous of their wives' love-affair with the God they so desperately need to love as well. This is occasionally the case with some women, too.

Evangelist John Smith observes:

> *Few atheists appear to have arrived at their conclusions by purely intellectual progression. Most harbour an innate anger against the God they so outspokenly deny.*[3]

In a rural parish a woman, Jane, came to see me because her marriage was experiencing great stress. Her husband, Bob, had 'switched off' from the relationship and was all-consumed with his farm, his golf and his boat. Jane was very aware of her own contribution to the breakdown; she had the capacity to nag and was sick of farm life — a fact that Bob knew well. However, she was still desperately in love with him.

After the first session, we agreed that the only way to move forward was for both of them to see me together.

Jane would ask Bob to come with her next time, though she thought her chances of his agreeing were not good. A week later, she rang me to say that he wouldn't cooperate. I saw her once more on her own.

A month later, with the situation worse, Jane arrived at my doorstep feeling quite desperate. We agreed that a casual note to him from me asking him to come along might work, but that he may already see me as the 'enemy' on her side. I wrote Bob this note:

> *Dear Bob:*
> *I'd like to encourage you and Jane to make the time to come and see me to talk over your family situation. It's so much easier to see the picture if I get both sides of the story and I'd like to hear yours. I stress that all this is completely confidential. Please do come, even if you feel a bit reluctant. We only need about an hour. . .*

When Bob received the note, he read it and immediately tore it into pieces in front of his wife and exclaimed, 'I'd rather our marriage collapsed in a screaming heap than go and see him!' It did.

Who taught us this stuff? Why is it that in just about every other department of life we acknowledge that there are people who can help, but not in relationships? When Bob's tractor breaks down, he knows a mechanic who can fix it. When Bob's son breaks his leg, he knows a doctor who can plaster it. When Bob's hay bailer gives up the ghost, he's got a team of neighbours to come and help. . . Yet when Bob's marriage is on the rocks, he says, 'It's *my* way or no way.' Who sold us the lie that we are automatically experts at our own marriages?

Maybe it has something to do with 'Rule number 7' (see last chapter): 'Don't show your feelings. To admit you are wrong is a sign of weakness.' Alongside the Protestant work ethic is the White-Anglo-Saxon-Protestant reserve, the stiff-upper-lip syndrome that has taught particularly men the lie that we must button-up our feelings, never admit defeat and certainly never cry.

Jack Dominian's comments are relevant here:

> *A feature of the companionship marriage is the need to be in touch with one another, to communicate effectively. In the first intimate relationship between child and parents, communication was entered into on the basis of touch and the expression of feelings. In the second intimate experience of marriage, couples — and particularly wives — want a similar experience of communication in terms of touch and affection.*
>
> *The difficulty here is often encountered by men whose physical contact is sexual and whose only form of communication is the expression of reason. There is thus often in marriage the conflict whereby the wife is in Jungian terms an intuitive, feeling person and the husband communicates in terms of intellect and reason.*
>
> *In practice, the wife complains that her husband does not talk to her, does not express loving feelings. He is perplexed and says to her that she 'knows' he loves her, he does not need to tell her so: but she does not know without active expression on his part, and so the conflict continues.*
>
> *The inability to express affection is particularly important when one of the spouses is markedly starved of love. Such a wife or husband needs to have a lot of affection shown to them. They need to be shown marked recognition, the feelings of being wanted and appreciated. When the spouse expresses these positive feelings all is well, but when the partner cannot do so, then the deprived individual feels unwanted and rejected and may seek affection outside the marriage.*
>
> *The inability to express angry feelings may rest on the basis of fear, the fear that if one is angry then the other person, in this case the spouse, will retaliate or reject one for good. Fear of anger resides in many people, the result of which is that they remain silent when they feel frustrated*

and angry; these feelings accumulate and one day burst into a mammoth explosion which takes everybody by surprise.

The failure to mobilise anger may be associated with the mobilisation of guilt feelings which are extremely painful. The inability to express feelings may have a genetic basis, because men are affected more often than women, or they may be socially conditioned, or it may be the result of the child not seeing the parents express feelings to each other.[4]

I thank God that I had a father who was not afraid to show me affection — even in public sometimes, which was a bit much at the age of fifteen in front of my mates! Every morning in my late teens, he would wake me up with a cup of tea and a kiss on the back of my neck. I feared his wrath, but I cherished his genuine, hands-on warmth and care. I saw my father cry — desperately, once. He had been hurt to the core by a superior and was in spiritual agony. I felt proud that he was *strong* enough to cry.

Twenty years after this event, I watched a man at the end of a funeral service weeping so audibly over a dear male friend who was now dead. His tears wet his wife's shoulder as everyone was leaving the church and I heard her say to him, 'Come on, Geoff, be strong, be strong.' I leaned over to her, smiled, and said, 'He is, he is.' I was moved to tears as well!

Jesus, too, was strong enough to cry. In John 11 (in the shortest and perhaps one of the most profound verses in the Bible) we read, 'Jesus wept' — and he did so over a beloved male friend.

The apparent 'toughness' of never crying goes with the saying, 'Never admit defeat.' The grace to say, 'I'm sorry' could save many a marriage, many a business and many a government. We will explore this dilemma more fully in chapter 7. Suffice for the present to offer this gem:

LET'S BACK DOWN

'And does that mean,' the interviewer asks, 'that you have backed down?'

'Certainly not!' retorts the interviewee, 'Never! My organisation has not backed down, we have no intention of backing down and, rather than back down, we'll bring the state to its knees, the country to ruin and the world to. . .'

You've heard those interviews, haven't you? It could be boss versus union, government versus opposition, state versus commonwealth. Even husband versus wife. The variations are endless, but the scenario follows the same old pattern:

> *First movement — confrontation. Hard words are said (but not heard) by both sides.*
> *Second movement — stalemate. Sulks all round.*
> *Third movement — compromise. Softer words are spoken (and listened to) and commonsense prevails.*
> *Fourth movement — all quiet on the Western Front.*

Danger is averted and no more is heard except, of course, the above interview. 'Back down?' they say, 'Certainly not, never, under no circumstances, over our collective dead bodies, etc. etc. etc.'

Now, as an experienced backing-downer from way back, I can never understand why people don't claim to back down. Why, I wonder, don't we get fewer of the above type of interviews and more which go like: 'Back down? Of course, we backed down. We had another look at what our opponents were saying and saw there was some truth in it, so, yes, we backed down. And if our opponents say they thought of it first, it's a downright lie. It was our idea to back down. What's more, we want to be the first to apologise for any inconvenience we may have caused. . .'

I'm willing to bet that any leader who took this sort of line on everything except matters of absolute principle (i.e. about one case in a million) would win any contest hands down. You don't believe me? Then tell me, given the choice between voting for the man who's always right, who never backs down, and the one who's as fallible as both of us and who isn't afraid to say, 'Sorry, but I goofed that one,' wouldn't you opt for number two? Yes, I thought so. Why? Because we know backing down is often a sign of strength, not of weakness.

Why? Because when it came to the crunch, God backed down, so to speak. He was truly God, yet he became truly man. Perfectly sinless, he was made sin for us. Pure Spirit, yet he was made flesh. Now there's backing down for you. God for a time becomes a slave. That's backing down with brass knobs on.

Paul says that Jesus didn't see his Godhead as something to be 'snatched at'. It was his by right, so he didn't have to grab at it. At the same time, he didn't hang on to it like grim death. For the good of mankind, he let go of it. He backed down. And he went on backing down all the way to the cross. Absolutely innocent, yet uncomplainingly accepted the verdict of guilty. So that those who were guilty might be declared innocent.

Yep, give me the bloke who knows when to back down.

Because when he does go forward, you know he's the bloke worth following.[5]

'For this reason a man shall leave his father and mother and be joined to his wife, and the two shall become one.'

Ephesians 5, verse 31

MARRIAGE

A wedding is a great society event, and lots of plans go into making the wedding day a memorable occasion for everyone.

The trouble is that society tends to place the couple on the top of the mountain on their wedding day, with very little care and concern about what happens next. And if you're on top of the mountain on your wedding day, there's only one way to go from then on. Down. If only people would concentrate a bit harder on the marriage and not the wedding — and there's a difference. Hopefully, about sixty years!

I like to think that on your wedding day you get the provisions for the mountain climb, the spiked shoes, the ropes, the special tools and supplies, and then you're off. And you'll have the occasional rock-slide, you'll take the wrong precipice, you'll have to rest and take stock of the situation, but slowly you'll be getting higher.

3

Failure to put in the hard work

MOST PEOPLE HAVE A SUPERFICIAL VIEW both of engagement and of marriage. Cultural, mythical and traditional expectations are attached to these two highly popular institutions which have very little resemblance to reality.

✠ Working things out during the engagement

There is more scandal today over a broken engagement than a broken marriage. 'Thou shalt not break thine engagement' could well be the eleventh commandment. Why? Because when you get engaged, you are seen as locked in to marriage. That is why many couples talk about getting engaged at a future date, perhaps months away, because they know they'll be seen to be locked in then.

Yet it is only when a couple become engaged that they will usually approach someone who will talk about preparation for this big step they are planning to make. This is highly commendable, of course, but the chances of a couple re-evaluating their situation after announcing their engagement are diminished by the fact that they are already fixed on a path to the altar in the eyes of their family and friends.

Nevertheless, the person they approach, usually the officiant, will — it is hoped — encourage them to take a real look at each other before the wedding rather than through the rose-coloured glasses given to them by a society which, by and large, sees the wedding as the mountain top.

I have seen invited guests quite horrified, some for months, when a wedding is called off. They ask questions like, 'What will they do with the engagement presents?' — never minding about the wisdom and courage of the couple concerned, let alone support for their decision not to go ahead. I have counselled a number of married couples who realised *before* their wedding day that they were not right for each other, but who have gone through with it simply not to disappoint their relations and guests.

By the time separation comes along — and this is sometimes only months after the wedding — the trauma is less because of the sense of inevitability in the air and the greater social acceptance of divorce. Yet the step of marriage has involved such a high commitment of persons, of possessions, of minds, bodies and spirits, even before the arrival of children who make the situation much more critical and distressing.

It's supposed to be the other way round! Would that there be many more broken engagements and less broken marriages. Sadly, the former are surprisingly few, the latter frighteningly too many.

Instead of the engagement being a time for serious exploration and evaluation with a view to a lifetime relationship in marriage, it is seen to be merely a period during which various preparations are made for the *wedding*. These include booking the reception and the church, arranging invitations, getting fittings and having functions such as 'pantry showers' and 'bucks' parties'. While all these preparations and traditions may be enjoyable and important, they are not the real substance of a good marriage — this actually involves realistic expectations, communication, conflict resolution, financial management, leisure planning and other related skills. Many of these skills can be developed in a relationship long before the wedding day. The engagement, hopefully at least nine months, is a good period to do some of this preparation, albeit in between all the arrangements!

Fortunately, I am finding that many more couples today do expect some kind of preparation for the marriage and not just the wedding. This can prevent the isolated 'mountain top' experience that a wedding can be if we allow only the traditions of society to impose a very narrow set of expectations upon us. These traditions also give a false interpretation to the role of the person who officiates at the wedding ceremony.

I use the word 'officiant' deliberately. Whether at a church or civil wedding, the couple themselves are the 'celebrants'. They celebrate the sacrament of marriage both on their wedding day and then every day of their married lives. I emphasise this not to split hairs, but to make it quite clear that the couple themselves, no-one else, 'carry the can' for their action. This is another good reason why they should say their own vows rather than repeat them after the officiant. The officiant doesn't marry them!

As the reflection on page 36 suggests, the problem of a wedding that is seen as the mountain top experience is that, once the honeymoon is over, there is only one way to go — down. Either that or the couple may think, unrealistically, that they will stay on a high, not recognising that their wedding rings are no inoculation of instant success in marriage. In fact, sometimes almost overnight, one can be tempted to take the other for granted and invest less time building the relationship than they did before the marriage. Sadly, I often meet couples who see much less of each other in marriage than they did in courtship — apart from their sleeping hours together in the same bed.

I once said to two bank officers on their wedding day: 'I don't need to tell you both that the more you *invest* in your marriage, the more *interest* you will receive!' Good marriage is an art and like any art it has to be developed and refined; it doesn't happen overnight.

This chapter is about getting the horse before the cart. The 'horse' is the work of marriage: for anything that is worthwhile in life needs a great deal of working on. The 'cart' is the satisfaction and joy that flows from that work. Too many couples, perhaps unwittingly, place the cart before the horse. This is manifested not only in the 'false climax' that the wedding day can be, but also in the expectations that the average young couple have about their home.

Most new matrimonial homes I walk into today have everything! It certainly may not all be paid for, but one gets the feeling that the couple have already 'arrived'. Certainly, there is much more emphasis today on the accumulation of material assets to make a marriage allegedly secure than on the attainment of the social skills needed to make it work and endure.

✠ Working on the marriage

The remainder of this chapter deals with some positive ideas and images that can enable the work of marriage to be a pleasure and a joy in itself. What underlies all these ideas and images is the dynamic of love which is the basis of the second part of this book.

Neither person in a marriage should take it for granted that their love will continue to grow without a great deal of effort. The wedding day is not the end of courtship and discovery. How many marriages have failed for the neglect of these two things alone. Most of these people immediately joined the 'now we're married, dear' club and began quickly adhering to the rules described in the first chapter.

Courtship, wooing, reassurance must continue through all our married lives, albeit in changing guises. We must be lovers always. I don't think we can ever tell our partners that we love them too many times. Of course, our actions will speak the loudest when it comes to love, but verbalising it is very important. Over the years of our marriage, our love will mature and impart its fragrance in different ways. The analogy of a fire is helpful here.

❒ *The fireplace of love: a positive image of marriage*

When we meet and fall in love, it is rather like a fire when it is first lit. Small kindling and dry leaves make a spectacular sight and sound. We spend a lot of time talking together, playing together, doing the crazy, zany things of love. Some of our friends think we are mad. We are! Madly in love — and the whole world needs to hear about it. Try convincing young lovers that it's great to sit down for hours and hours reading books and listening to Bach organ preludes.

The early years can be more 'physical', too. My mother always felt quite disgusted with people 'forever fondling each other in public'! Young couples do tend to be more hands-on in this regard and that is quite normal. Someone even suggested to me on our honeymoon that for the first six months we should put a coin in a jar every time we made love and then, after that, take one out each time, with the idea that we would never empty the jar. After twenty years of marriage, I do believe we may have proved him wrong!

Once the early years of courtship and marriage are over, the spectacular side of love diminishes in the growing security and stability of home and family life, for children are usually on the scene by now. This is a busy and demanding period for couples akin to the more deliberate and careful placing of larger pieces of wood upon the fire so that it will begin to establish a good heat base. We notice at this time that the fire doesn't have the same cub-scout appeal any more, for scouts tend to leave their bonfires at the time when the fire is giving out less light, but perhaps much more heat.

Nevertheless, at this stage in the marriage, it is so important to regularly fuel the fire for, while the wood is larger, it burns through very quickly. Many couples experience difficulty after seven or eight years for this reason ('the seven-year itch'), for they have got used to things and, in the busyness of work and child-rearing, they have not taken time out to chop the wood.

However, in a healthy marriage, the feelings of security, contentment and fulfilment are growing — and a sense of pride in what is being accomplished. The couple express their love for each other in more refined terms: supportive enquiry and encouragement, flowers, a dinner for two, a fun-time with the children, a 'naughty weekend' away. . . The fire is firmly established now and is beginning to fill the home with its warmth.

It is important at this stage for the couple to be still very aware of each other's needs as well as their children's, for many a marriage has collapsed after the children have left home because the couple have nothing left to live for — they have lived for too long mainly for their children. This is another example of putting the cart before the horse. The horse in this case should always be the love of the husband and wife. There can be no greater contribution to the health, welfare and happiness of children than for their parents to show that they love each other very much.

My wife and I have some friends who have a plaque on their mantelpiece with the inscription: *'The best thing a father can do for his children is to love their mother.'*

In the later years of marriage and long after the children have left home, the fire has changed its appearance quite markedly. Now, perhaps with just one large log, it provides a consistent, radiant heat and doesn't need stoking or refuelling for hours. The couple can bask in its heat, perhaps saying very few words — there is no need. They know each other through and through. There is a feeling of peace and completion. Yes, these two can read books for hours in each other's company and yet feel intimately at one. Most of the hard work and wood-chopping is behind, and the chimney is drawing sweetly. These are the halcyon days of marriage.

A lifetime of love, through good days and bad, has been fuelled and fanned by devotion, constancy, commitment and trust.

❒ *The Bible: a source of positive ideas about marriage*

Respect for each other must continue and grow through marriage — and deep consideration. We need to enable each other to grow and blossom into the fullness of the man and the woman God has created us to be.

Marriage as God intended it in creation can never be equated with the social institutionalisation of it in any given period of time. It is often the institutional form of marriage that some young people are rejecting today, not marriage as intended by the Creator. The Bible affirms that marriage is not some human option or alternative lifestyle but a divine creation, even when it is entered into without religious faith. But where there is faith, biblical models for good marriage abound.

The first important biblical principle of marriage is fidelity. One of the most profound statements about marriage in the Bible occurs in the letter to the Ephesians, where the writer says: 'This is a great mystery and I am applying it to Christ and the church' (Ephesians 5, verse 32). In *An Australian Prayer Book* (1978), the Marriage Preface states that marriage is the symbol of God's unending love for his people and of the union between Christ and his church.[1]

Anglican archbishop Keith Rayner has said: 'The great characteristic of Christ's relationship with his church is that of absolute faithfulness. He lived, ministered and died for us, his church, not because the church is good enough to deserve it, but because his love for the church is such that he remains faithful to it even when it fails him.'[2]

Fidelity can exist even when there has been a failure in the past by one or both parties. This faithfulness will be explored in the second half of this book. The quality of married fidelity will be such that when one partner is hurt, misunderstood or feels forsaken, he or she will not stand off waiting for an apology that may never come or an act of reassurance that may not be given, but will take the initiative personally to reconcile the relationship. Such was the way of Christ. The fidelity of husband and wife to each other is central to the understanding of marriage and this quality is to radiate outwards through the family circle into community and secular life.

It is never too early or too late to take a fresh glance at each other, in love, and to make changes if necessary in order to grow in companionship, faithfulness and strength. We may need to reassess our *attitudes*, for some of them may be detrimental to our relationships and to ourselves. An attitude is simply the way you 'lean'. Pilots know this, for in an aeroplane the 'attitude' is the tilt of the wingspan in relation to the horizon. A fixed attitude can often be a killer, whether in a 'plane, a marriage or in a business. We can change our attitudes as simply as changing gears in a car or finding another way up the mountain.[3]

A marriage certificate is rather like a driver's licence. You're out on the road (together) at last. But this piece of paper doesn't mean you're the world's perfect driver; it doesn't mean you're an expert at the wheel. It means that your journey has just begun and you may make quite a few mistakes along the way, but you've got sufficient skills and know how to get there in the end. However, right now you're wearing P-plates! You may find yourself speeding, cutting corners, overtaking in the wrong places and having the occasional bump (hopefully not a major prang), but eventually you'll become a better driver through your marriage. . . and *only* if you change some bad driving habits.

Don't forget that your marriage wagon needs regular servicing as well as fuel. The tyres can wear thin as well as the brakes. It won't take you very far unless you take good care of it. It is an investment and needs to be looked after and, when it is, it will take you travelling for a lifetime.

They don't hand out demerit points in marriages, but if they did, I'm sure we'd all have quite a few!

The second important biblical principle of marriage is mutual submission. This means being 'subject to *one another* out of reverence for Christ' (Ephesians 5, verse 21). This is another reason why so many marriages have come unstuck: we have come to regard as normal the opposite of being submissive. Our age is preoccupied with people's individual rights — the 'me generation'. However, there is an inherent danger with this worldview, particularly if it is kept in isolation. John Smith observes:

> *The Bible tells husbands to love their wives as Christ loves the church. That meant crucifixion for him, not opting out. I am staggered at the number of religious folk who are finding neat little words like 'incompatibility' as a basis*

> *for breaking marriages. I seriously doubt there is such a thing as incompatibility. There are poor choices, difficult options, less-than-ideal foundations of common interest — but lasting and fulfilling relationships are a matter of mutual commitment.*
>
> *Sometimes naturally conflicting relationships, if intelligently and compassionately worked through, make for more creative human endeavour. In the Western world, we are far more selfish and individualistic in our assessments. A Third World proverb says, 'Broken glass shines the brightest.' But in our culture, the proverb would read, 'If in danger of being shattered, get out now!'*[4]

Ephesians 5 calls on wives to be subject to their husbands, children to obey their parents and slaves to be obedient to their masters — and these statements, obviously set within the culture of their day, go against the grain for many people today.

But we can often fail to realise that *reverse* obligations are also set out in the same passage: 'Husbands, love your wives, just as Christ loved the church and gave himself up for her. . .' (Ephesians 5, verse 25).

And here's a tall order for the men: '. . .fathers, do not provoke your children to anger. . .' (Ephesians 6, verse 4). In other words, what is envisaged for the family is a pattern of relationships in which each person recognises responsibilities to the other. Many husbands and fathers forsake their role — wives and mothers, too — and the consequences have been clearly disastrous. Mutual submission is a must for *every* marriage, be it the traditional or modern egalitarian version.

The third important biblical principle is the corporateness of family life. The family is more than a collection of individuals who happen to live together: it is seen as a *whole*. The word 'family' has the same root as the word 'familiar'. Too many families just rush and rush about, doing their own frenetic thing and having very little time together — communicating, talking, growing in love together. This is very damaging. The Bible upholds marriage and the family as the *basic* unit which needs to be one that is filled with honour, respect and deep, forgiving love (see Colossians 3, verses 12 to 15). But every family needs to make the space and time for this.

These principles may not be the in thing today, but they are the substance of true community. As husbands and wives, the words for most of us on our wedding day were that we would 'forsake all others' as long as we both should live.

All of us need to look at where our real priorities lie. There are too many shattered dreams out there that are due to other priorities getting so diabolically in the way of our marriages and families. We need to be careful: our lifestyle alone may be fostering breakdown, as the following reflections observe:

GROWING TOGETHER

But speaking the truth in love, we must grow up in every way into him who is the head, into Christ, from whom the whole body, joined and knit together by every ligament with which it is equipped, as each part is working properly, promotes the body's growth in building itself up in love.[5]

THE BREAKFAST BAR

We have a breakfast bar at home — a bench in the kitchen with stools around it. Many people have them in their homes these days, because they're so convenient. They have storage space underneath, they're good for preparing food, and are so handy for eating purposes.

Like many other gadgets in the kitchen, time is saved with our breakfast bar, so that we can get on with the rest of the day. The trouble is, we don't get to talk very much together. . . it's not the sort of place where you sit for very long, and the dining table is only used when we have guests for dinner.

Lord, convenience is killing so many families; don't let it happen to mine. That breakfast bar, like our television set, can stifle communication, can stop us talking, praying, loving, growing up together.

Help us and other families to see the need to make time together to enjoy each other. After all, what are families for?

Part B:
Marriages built on solid rock

One Thing At Least

One thing at least I understand
Practically from the start,
That loving must be learnt by heart
If it's to be any good.

It isn't in the flash of thunder,
But in the silent power to give —
A habit into which we live
Ourselves, and grow to be a wonder.

Some like me are slow to learn:
What's plain can be mysterious still.
Feelings alter, fade, return,

But love stands constant in the will:
It's not alone the touching, seeing;
It's how to meet the other's being.

James McAuley, 1917–1976

4

Love yourself unconditionally

THIS SECOND PART OF THE BOOK is about the many-faceted diamond of love and its force for our married and family lives.

As mentioned earlier, one of the factors leading to marital and family stress today is low self-esteem. The society in which we live, while geared to high achievement and productivity, manifests acute negativity.

In the workplace, most employers are quick to condemn, slow to praise. During a time of staff cutbacks and high unemployment, many are expecting more than their pound of flesh because they have the bargaining power. Conversations in the office are more likely to dwell on failure in business than on success stories — they make for more gossip value. Affairs and broken relationships take the same spotlight.

I find myself counselling more people suffering from feelings of defeat, depression and suicidal tendencies than I did twenty years ago. Some of these people are high school students who are not handling the pressure to achieve — so much greater in the nineties than in the sixties when I was a student.

In those days, senior high school graduates had the world as their oyster. I understand that one in six young people between the ages of fifteen and nineteen seriously contemplates suicide and that, after road accidents, suicide is the greatest killer in this age group.

Behind all these statistics, there is a false and dangerous general assumption held by believers and non-believers alike that the Christian God approves of those who categorically disapprove of themselves while exalting others. So low self-esteem can't be such a bad thing.

While the Christian gospel has much to say about humility and placing the interests of others above our own, the second great commandment is to love your neighbour *as yourself* (Mark 12, verse 31). If we are meant to love our neighbour as ourselves, how do we love ourselves? And if we don't particularly love ourselves, it may well be that we aren't doing a very good job on our neighbours.

The Christian gospel, in fact, teaches that in God's sight each one of us is infinitely precious. Right at the beginning of creation, God beheld what he had made in his own image, after his own likeness — namely, our humanity — and he blessed it (Genesis 1, verses 26 to 28). Our sin has got in the way of his plan, but his love remains unconditional. He loves us more than we dare imagine!

Jesus picked this up in his Sermon on the Mount, when he said:

> *Therefore I tell you, do not worry about your life, what you will eat or what you will drink, or about your body, what you will wear. Is not life more than food, and the body more than clothing? Look at the birds of the air; they neither sow nor reap nor gather into barns, and yet your heavenly Father feeds them. Are you not of more value than they? And can any of you by worrying add a single hour to your span of life? And why do you worry about clothing? Consider the lilies of the field, how they grow; they neither toil nor spin, yet I tell you, even Solomon in all his glory was not clothed like one of these.*
>
> *But if God so clothes the grass of the field, which is alive today and tomorrow is thrown into the oven, will he not*

much more clothe you — you of little faith? Therefore, do not worry, saying 'What will we eat?' or 'What will we drink?' or 'What will we wear?' For it is the Gentiles who strive for all these things; and, indeed, your heavenly Father knows that you need all these things. But strive first for the kingdom of God and his righteousness, and all these things will be given to you as well.

So do not worry about tomorrow, for tomorrow will bring worries of its own. Today's trouble is enough for today.[1]

We need to affirm ourselves and affirm others in the business of daily life. It is too easy to destroy people: 'the tongue is a fire. . . with it we bless the Lord and Father, and with it we curse those who are made in the likeness of God' (James 3, verses 6 and 9). Many seem to be very effective in this regard. Some even enjoy seeing people put down, put in their place, biting the dust.

The singer, Whitney Houston, sang a popular song in the mid eighties, *The Greatest Love of All*. While I don't quite concur with the label 'greatest' — the greatest love is the love of God — the song beautifully highlights the need to love yourself.

As I reflected on this song, I was reminded of the Book of Deuteronomy where Moses speaks to the people of Israel about the first commandment: 'You and your children and your children's children may fear the Lord your God all the days of your life, and keep all his decrees and his commandments that I am commanding you, so that all your days may be long' (Deuteronomy 6, verse 2). There is a real concern to pass through the generations the teaching, discipline and love of God to our children and our children's children.

In Whitney's song, we hear the words:

I believe that children are our future;
Teach them well and let them lead the way.
Show them all the beauty they possess inside;
Give them a sense of pride to make it easier —
Let the children's laughter remind us how we used to be.

I know I don't laugh as much as I did when I was a child; more's the pity. I tend to take life much too seriously — I wasn't like that once. One of the reasons is my low self-esteem. I'm still trying to find where it came from, because it's baggage I collected somewhere and it's baggage I don't need to carry any more.

A *sense* of pride is a very different thing to the *sin* of pride. Self-esteem is a very different thing to selfishness or self-exaltation. We truly need to own the difference — to gird ourselves in self-esteem and be easier on ourselves, our children and our children's children.

As you read this, what do you really think about yourself? Jesus calls you 'the light of the world' and he wants your light to shine (Matthew 5, verses 14 and 16). He doesn't want you to be anxious about your life — you are precious in his sight.

What is your image of yourself? What do you *really* believe about yourself — in your deepest, soul-searching moments? Your attitude matters a great deal in this area, too: your attitude to yourself and your attitude to others. You can have positive and negative attitudes, but they really only become so when you set yourself goals.

The same can be said of your character, your personality. For example, being a bit withdrawn is not positive or negative until you explore your goal. If you want to manage a successful nightclub, being withdrawn could be a negative thing. But if you are inclined to research work, spending many hours in isolation, it could well be a positive thing. An attitude is simply the way you *lean*.

We can, in fact, change our attitudes by changing our picture of ourselves or our goals in life. The same can be said of our relationship with others. Of a quiet, withdrawn person, we might be tempted to say: 'You don't mix that well, do you?. . . You're not exactly the life of the party!' — which is a negative attitude. Instead, we might observe: 'You're a great listener; when I talk to you I always feel you're really tuning in to what I say' — which is a positive attitude and builds that person up, doesn't put them down.

Many people have a negative self-image. Sometimes, that image is produced via the influence of others, often in childhood. If a person is called stupid by someone, that information is recorded in the mind. Every time that person vividly imagines the experience of being called stupid, it is as good as if it were happening again. The subconscious mind doesn't know the difference between something real and something we *imagine* to be real. If we're called foolish enough times, we can end up believing it even when it isn't true.

Jesus had some strong words to say about this: 'If you say "you fool", you will be liable to the hell of fire' (Matthew 5, verse 22). He knew just what this negative, damaging information could do to a person. If you forever tell your child: 'Your room looks like a pigsty; clean it up, *you messy child!*', that child will end up believing that she is a messy person. Far better to say: 'Please hang your clothes up; you know how to keep your room tidy.' The child begins to believe: 'I'm tidy.'

You may be carrying a lot of beliefs about yourself which may not be true at all. In your self-talk[2] — the things you keep believing about yourself — you may be undermining your real self-worth and the many strengths that you possess. Think of the things you often say about yourself. Do any of the following statements ring bells?

'How could I be so stupid?'
'There I go again — getting it wrong!'
'What's the matter with me anyway?'
'I can't do anything right!'
'This is going to be one of those days. . .'

The cartoon character, Ziggy, is the born loser. One of my favourite captions goes something like this: 'How come every time opportunity knocks, I'm out the back putting out the garbage?' The problem is that a lot of us really do believe this stuff! This is the *real* garbage.

Who told you to hold onto this rubbish? Most of it is simply your own reinforced negative self-talk and it can ruin your life. You don't have to be like this. You can change your beliefs about yourself, because beliefs are not necessarily the same as truth. You can learn to love yourself because, until you have genuine self-worth, you cannot love your neighbour as yourself. That neighbour includes your own husband or wife, your children and your parents.

What are your real strengths?

Here's a 'Self-Love Exercise'. . . Get a pen and paper and write down some nice things about yourself — things you're good at, your gifts. Remember the old television show, *This is Your Life*? Why not call your exercise, *This is* My *Life*? Spoil yourself with compliments and praise for a change! Under that list, write down some attitudes you know you can change about yourself — the way you lean towards or away from yourself in various situations: your work. . . your boss. . . your study. . . your family. . . your life. Change some of that self-talk.

Then, think of the changes you could make in the way you talk to others, especially the members of your family. Do you put people down or build them up in the way you react to things that threaten or displease you? You might like to use two headings: 'The old Me' and 'The new Me'.

Here's an example that many people say about themselves: 'I don't like Mondays'. Just imagine the way that statement affects national productivity on Mondays! You could change it to 'I like the challenge of a new week' and then see how that affects your performance.

I once put together a book of Graces to be said at mealtimes. For a Monday morning, I wrote:

With this food, dear Lord, delight us;
Preserve us, Lord, from Mondayitis!

Actually, in my present work I have Mondays off, which is great!

If we can begin to eradicate from our marriages and families negative self-talk and negative attitudes to each other, we will soon feel a new confidence and be ready to stand tall alongside each other in love.

Daily affirmation of one another's gifts is a great habit to get into. 'I believe in you. . .'; 'You're good at that. . .'; 'I know that you can do it. . .'; 'You're the one for the job'. We can show each other in the words of that song the beauty we possess inside — and feel a sense of pride in all that we are and all that we do.

St Paul said: 'I can do all things through him who strengthens me' (Philippians 4, verse 13). The source of all that we are and all that we do is God. Our self-love can be the reflection of the unity and love that exists in the Godhead, the love of the Father with the Son in the Holy Spirit. It is that love which said: 'Let us make humankind in *our* image, according to *our* likeness' (Genesis 1, verse 26).

The Psalm writer puts it like this:

For it was you who formed my inward parts;
you knit me together in my mother's womb.
I praise you, for I am fearfully and wonderfully made.
Wonderful are your works;
that I know very well.
My frame is not hidden from you,
when I was being made in secret,
Intricately woven in the depths of the earth.
Your eyes beheld my unformed substance.
In your book were written
all the days that were formed for me,
when none of them as yet existed.[4]

Learn to love yourself and you will then be ready to love others with an unconditional love.

Love is not a feeling.
Love is a decision.
John Powell

5

Equip yourself for the journey of love

IN SPITE OF A SUSTAINED LEVEL OF BREAKDOWN in marriage and the acceptance of alternative lifestyles, the conventional family (the nuclear family) is still regarded as the norm today. But in fact, this 'norm' is a minority group and more than half all households in Australia are childless (including retired people), while another large percentage have only one parent or one biological parent at home.

There is at the moment a swing against alternative lifestyles in the absence of any one viable, superior model — back to the call for traditional family life. While this is commendable on biblical grounds alone, things can never be the same as they were forty years ago. For example, the two-income family is here to stay for a long time yet. Over fifty per cent of married women in Australia are now income earners.

Apart from the obvious economic benefits to the family, the employment of married women gives them a financial independence they never had in the fifties. Therefore, separation and divorce are more economically possible in contrast to a time when economic necessity and the threat of social stigma kept many marriages together. It follows that the quality of modern marriages must be more sound if they are to survive and, hopefully, flourish.

This chapter offers some ideas that couples can develop in the building of equipment and skills for good marriage. Most of these ideas aren't original, but they work. A list of resource agencies can be found in Appendix A at the end of this book.

In putting these ideas together, I am particularly grateful to *Prepare-Enrich Incorporated*, whose resources I use regularly as a *Prepare* Counsellor, and the *Marriage Encounter* movement.

When Deborah and I were preparing for the birth of our first child, William, I was struck by something quite ironic. We attended eight or nine ante-natal sessions at which there were wall-to-wall husbands with pregnant wives. All of these were eager to know about everything from birthing-breathing techniques and changing nappies to breast versus bottle feeding. The men wouldn't have missed these for the world, yet many might have balked at even two or three sessions of marriage preparation.

Having babies (and making them!) is something quite natural for most couples. I am sure that, if we hadn't attended all these sessions, William would still have come into the world quite healthy and happy, but it was certainly good to be prepared.

Getting married and staying married, however, are things that don't come naturally at all. And children represent just one aspect in the whole gamut of married life and responsibilities. It is crucial to healthy marriage that every aspect be examined by way of preparation, prior to the wedding.

I look forward to the day when there will be strong 'ante-nuptial' eagerness amongst couples to find out and dialogue about all they can. The *Prepare* material is certainly a good resource to begin this process.

✠ Develop communication skills

John Powell describes communication as 'the secret of staying in love' in a book of the same title.[1]

If a couple are open to each other in free communication, many other aspects of married life will be dealt with effectively. Good communication skills include careful listening, engaging dialogue and discussion, understanding the unspoken and encouragement.

❒ *First, listen carefully*

In listening to what our partner is trying to say, we need to be in touch with our partner's feelings even more than with ideas or viewpoints. Ideas and viewpoints may indicate our persuasions in life, but they are not the unique thing about us — they are not the substance of what we share in love.

Our feelings are what make us truly knowable, writes John Powell:

> *My feelings are like my fingerprints, the colour of my eyes, and the sound of my voice: unique to me and unrepeatable in anyone else. To know me you must know my feelings. And only when you know me through dialogue at any moment of my life will you be able to understand my ideas, preferences and intentions, shared in discussion.*[2]

Often in marriage we can make decisions without discovering the feelings behind the making of those decisions. The comment 'She was hearing me, but she wasn't listening to what I was saying' is a statement about feelings rather than information. Communication breakdown can often occur when two people become so determined to get across their own views that they fail to understand each other's feelings.

It is a good idea to get into the habit of asking our

partner, 'How do you feel about. . .?' We then need to listen carefully and perhaps request further information about the subject so that we are quite clear.

❐ *Second, engage in dialogue and discussion*
Most families talk a lot; fewer make the time to engage in dialogue and discussion that has the deliberate intention of building understanding, trust and care. In courtship, many couples, often unconsciously, become quite skilled at this art, yet very quickly lose it when they are under the one roof of marriage.

Simply finding ten minutes each day to enter into a meaningful dialogue can transform the quality of a marriage. Such conversation can include:

* *The good opener:* 'How's your day been?' Share together the pleasant or not-so-pleasant events of the day, entering into each other's feelings.
* *The family schedule* for the days ahead, including the chores.
* *Sharing personal aspirations, doubts and needs.*
* *Decisions*, contracted or covenanted on a mutual basis.
* *On-going problems* and issues over which there has been disagreement. It is not always possible to solve a problem, but it is dangerous to try and bury a problem that is still alive. As John Powell writes:

> *Two people in love can continue to deepen in their affection for each other while holding opposite opinions in almost any area of life. These contrary intellectual persuasions do not become an obstacle to love until one or both the parties feels emotionally threatened.*[3]

You may wish to offer some of these things in a simple prayer together. I like the old motto: 'A family that prays together stays together.' I have rarely seen it proved wrong.

❒ *Third, seek to understand the unspoken*

This is sometimes referred to as 'non-verbal' communication. Understanding comes not only through careful attention to spoken words, but also in the discernment of 'body language'. In fact, facial expressions and gestures will often give us more information than words, or even cancel out what has been said! If we perceive that our partner is saying one thing but feeling another, then we can gently check it out and invite response: 'You don't seem to be very happy about that arrangement. Do you want to talk about it?' We may or may not be correct in our perception.

❒ *Fourth, provide encouragement*

I have mentioned earlier that reassurance is very important in marriage. Just because we have each other's love doesn't mean that we shouldn't offer regular expressions of respect, value and appreciation. I believe that if we are truly mindful of the little things in life, then the big things will take care of themselves.

A bunch of flowers on a wedding anniversary is the 'right thing' to do, but flowers on a 'nothing day' work wonders! Words of gratitude, compliments about food and dress, expressions of pride in accomplishments — all these things can speak volumes to our partner who may otherwise feel taken for granted.

✠ Develop conflict resolution skills

If there is real openness to each other in these four

important areas of communication then, when conflict occurs as it inevitably will from time to time, there will be the skills to deal with it effectively.

A worthwhile exercise in conflict is to put aside time together to write down individually the issues as we see them and then share them in dialogue without challenging each other's rights to raise them. Most conflicts arise from emotional factors and can be dealt with constructively once we are tuned into each other's feelings.

The next step is to list together as many possible solutions to the central issue or problem. Discuss each one while making sure feelings are respected. Cross off the solutions unacceptable to either or both. Put the others in order of preference. Then, agree on one trial solution, discussing how each of you is to try and make it work. Agree on a future date to assess how it is going and whether any of the other solutions might work better.

❒ *First, resolving personality differences*

There are always going to be things we like very much and things we dislike about each other's personalities. The dislikes can have the effect of compounding over the years if we let them. This is because we can tend to overlook minor annoyances in courtship and early marriage. They seem insignificant in comparison to the joy and positive feelings we have in so many areas. Perhaps unconsciously, we believe that our love will 'ride over' these things. Instead, we can become quite resentful about them, wondering why our partner won't change. Our partner in turn may feel hurt that we don't love them and accept them as they are.

Some habits may be annoying but trivial, nevertheless. My wife almost always puts the toilet roll on the holder with the paper coming down against the wall. At one house we lived in, this literally had the effect of stripping the paint and plaster off the wall! Then there is the old chestnut where one partner squeezes the toothpaste at the top to the annoyance of those who know better! There will be many areas of behaviour akin to this that simply demand greater acceptance, tolerance and often a sense of humour. If no real harm is being done by some kind of behaviour, then there is probably no need for change.

But there are bound to be areas where personality issues do pose the threat of harm to the relationship. How do we handle these? In some cases, change should, can and will occur. In others, it may be that our *attitude* to our partner's perceived problem will have to change. This can occasionally have the effect in the long term of stimulating a change in our partner, too.

The *Prepare-Enrich* program offers some steps to take in negotiating change which need to be understood, accepted and put into practice carefully by both parties:

When asking for change in your partner:

* *Be careful* with, and loving and sensitive to, your partner. Avoid being angry and hurtful.
* *Be honest*, open and sincere, rather than denying what you feel and believe. Honesty does not have to be expressed with heat and anger. Tact is more important than brutal honesty.
* *Focus upon what you believe and feel* about the behaviour which concerns you. Don't attack the person; stay with an expression of your view of the activity or attitude which troubles you.
* *Listen to and understand your partner's reaction*. You have invited comment, so be ready to handle it well. Be open-minded, flexible and prepared to give ground.

When being asked to change by your partner:

* *Listen* and try to understand what your partner is saying. Concentrate on the issue.
* When you are sure you fully understand the issue, *express your reaction*, being loving and sensitive to your partner.
* *Remember, your partner values you enough to want to take down any barriers* which might be coming between you.[4]

Any 'balance of power' changes must be handled with kid gloves. Many marriages fail at this point because one partner is being left behind as the other, often the female, finds new purpose and makes more space for personal fulfilment. Carefully talking through each stage of change and respecting each other's individual needs can make this transition smoother.

Again, taking the time out to do an exercise along similar lines to the one suggested above in dealing with conflict may be very helpful. More often, a personal change of attitude, adopting skills to cope positively with our partner's problem, is more fruitful. Here are two examples:

1. *Her lack of affection*

John really gets frustrated because Anne very rarely shows him hands-on affection, as distinct from 'sex'. He longs for Anne to put her arms around him when he comes home from work — to be more warm to him in public, too.

In the past, John has got quite upset about it and has repeatedly asked Anne why she is like that and why she can't be more demonstrative. This has only served to push Anne further away. She has often told John that there is no point in doing it unless she feels she wants to and she rarely does — it just isn't 'her'.

John has learned not to be as frustrated at the lack of affection: first, by recognising that this isn't to do with him personally — it's just the way Anne is — and second, by recognising his positive feelings about her loving behaviour towards him in a number of other areas. Anne always wants to know how his day has been. She dresses beautifully and she knows it appeals to him; he often receives clothes and other gifts from her just because she was thinking of him. They have a very enjoyable sex life.

The bonus is that Anne now does have more displays of affection towards him, too, but he tries not to show too much excitement, just in case she backs off!

2. *His shocking moods*

Whenever George had a hard day at work, his wife and children really got a hammering that night. Not that he got stuck into them personally; he would just 'blast off' in front of them a lot.

This had a most unsettling effect upon everyone. George could see that effect even while he continued to let forth in his selfish tantrum. Lorraine used to yell back at him and say things like, 'Leave your work at the office if you can't just come home and relax; we're sick of your constant bad moods!' But this used to make George worse and he would think that Lorraine didn't care about his disappointments. It had the effect of fuelling his fury even more.

Lorraine and the children have now learned some simple skills to deal with this. The children usually make a point of being in their rooms playing or doing homework when Dad comes home. Lorraine makes sure that she is occupied with something that reminds George that she, too, has had a busy day. She then enquires about his day, giving him her whole attention for a few minutes. The tantrums are shorter and less frequent because Lorraine has changed her attitude and the new skills have had a 'defusing' effect upon George. The children come out when the coast is clear and the family settle down to some meaningful and enjoyable conversation. George still has his moody moments, but they are nowhere near as bad as before.

We may not be able to change our partner's bad habits, but we can change our attitudes which may well sometimes be the catalyst for change in them, too.

You may like to make some space right now to see if there are any experiences in your relationship that could be handled in this way.

❐ *Second, resolving sexual and emotional differences*

Most husbands and wives do experience differences in sexual and emotional makeup and needs. The best way to work through these is to talk about them openly together.

Generally speaking, a man can switch on to sex very quickly, whereas a woman requires an ambience enhanced by the connectedness of the whole relationship. One partner may be more into a variety of sexual activity than the other. This very important area in marriage, therefore, needs to be given the time for understanding, accepting or carefully rejecting particular requests for sexual pleasure.

The satisfaction of the other before the self should always be the goal for both. If your partner is reluctant about something that would bring you pleasure, then to refrain from that activity is an expression of your love; ceasing to request it is also a sign of growth. Long-term emotional hurt due to activity which has never really been happily consented to can cause enormous damage to a relationship.

You may have a very giving partner who is trying to please you in every possible way. Be careful not to exploit this; check it out together.

Again, adopting skills to deal positively with the different needs you and your partner may have can work wonders in the sexual and emotional department. Furthermore, the couple who are able to share freely in private the things that enhance their lovemaking will be more able to share with their children the joys and responsibilities of sex rather than making it to be seen as something either clinical or crude. A little more will be said about this below.

✠ Make plans and set goals

Many marriages come unstuck because the couple get into a rut. The days, weeks, months and years tick by and it can seem that we're just going through the motions of married and family life without much purpose and without too many genuine encounters. Then, if financial hardship or illness strike, we can almost feel holed below the waterline and that our love boat is sinking.

This is a time of great economic change that is having a devastating impact upon families. Marriage breakdown due to financial stress is at an all-time high. Some people have had to sell their homes, cars and possessions to pay off bad debts. Others aren't coping with retrenchment in the midst of life with a large family still to feed, clothe and educate. Youth unemployment is critical and the government has held a summit on this issue alone.

Wise planning and goal-setting can provide couples with a strong sense of direction, durability and purpose, regardless of external pressures upon their marriage. Jesus told an excellent little parable that we can apply to this situation:

> *Everyone. . . who hears these words of mine and acts on them will be like a wise man who built his house on rock. The rain fell, the floods came, and the winds blew and beat on that house, but it did not fall, because it had been founded on rock. And everyone who hears these words of mine and does not act on them will be like a foolish man who built his house on sand. The rain fell, and the floods came, and the winds blew and beat against that house, and it fell — and great was its fall!* [5]

Later, we examine in depth the strong foundation of love, given to us in the example of Christ, upon which our marriages can build a secure, impenetrable fortress. For the present, we can use this parable for more practical purposes. What rock-solid strategies can we put into operation that will weather the storms of life around us?

Financial planning and budgeting is an area where such strategies can be applied. It is a great idea to sit down together with some paper and pens and see how your finances are working out and where you want them to go. Most people are more than capable of living within their means, provided that there is open and honest discussion about *all* the finances, and mutual agreement as to their expenditure.

The first thing to do is put all your cards on the table and draw up a list with two columns headed 'assets' and 'liabilites'. Any bank would be happy to assist you with forms that are usually drawn up for loans. They make a good resource for this exercise.

With this list, you will quickly see whether you are living within or beyond your means. Now move on to draw up the next twelve month's budget, including a component for savings and emergencies. And don't forget a holiday allocation. Before commencing your annual budget, however, please consider what I believe to be the secret recipe to financial happiness today.

We all need to make a big distinction between our *wants* and our *needs*. Put down those two headings and honestly appraise your present situation. Designer label clothes don't last any longer than off-the-rack. Of course, post-season sales can indulge your wants at half the price if you must! Cask wine can save you heaps; keep the bottles for dinner parties. Bulk or plain label food is often as good or better than top dollar; and do your shopping with a full stomach. You may want a Merc in the garage, but a Holden will get you there in style.

Over the last few years, I have counselled a number of top executives who have gone to the wall because of the 1987 stockmarket crash and subsequent recession. Most have been amazed to find that it is possible to live very comfortably on $30 000 a year when some had been spending that kind of money on clothes, holidays and entertainment alone! They have simply worked very hard on separating out their wants from their needs and concentrating just on their needs.

Most of us can live more simply if we try. Remember that great catch-phrase they used for the Christmas Bowl Appeal one year: 'Live more simply that others may simply live'? One of the best teachers in the art of simplicity that I have come across after Jesus himself is Richard Foster. I thoroughly recommend his books, *Celebration of Discipline* and *Freedom of Simplicity*.[6] Simplicity is not only the secret to financial stability in a marriage. It can make us so aware of all the other good things in life as well. Most of us are more blessed than we think.

The next thing to do is to work out your long-term financial goals and the saving strategy you will need to meet them. There are a number of organisations that have experts in budget counselling and financial planning. The agencies listed in Appendix A of this book can refer you to them.

✠ Cultivate good leisure, food and sex

They say that variety is the spice of life. However, many marriages and families experience a stifling sameness about them when it comes to their togetherness and leisure time. It really is great fun to plan dining, leisure and entertainment activities. This can be conducted over the meal table with the children. (Sexual adventures, however, might best be planned in the bedroom!)

My children often write a menu just for an ordinary family meal in order to make it special. They get out the candles, at no prompting from Deborah or myself, turn off the lights and, in so doing, transform what could have been just another tummy-filling exercise at the end of a hard day into an intimate family celebration that is touched with a blessing.

We all need to be open to doing something different at least once a week, either at home or on an outing, and it needn't cost money.

Even our marital sex-life can become more like work than play. Husbands and wives need to be quite relaxed, honest and patient with each other in exploring techniques that will enhance this very special part of their lives. We refer to couples 'consummating' their marriage on their wedding night. The word means 'to complete' or 'to perfect'. There is nothing more humanly beautiful than to complete each other in this way when the day is over. But if you're on holidays, why wait until the evening? Have *fun*!

Nevertheless, always remember that sexual satisfaction is only one part of marriage and that a lot of couples for whom sex is not magic have been able to build strong, happy and fulfilling marriages based on other aspects of their relationship.

✠ Set aside time for family and friends

We also need to set aside specific quality time for our children that is intentionally father/mother and son/daughter orientated. I find that fathers in particular are often distant from their children. Pressure of business is one of the main excuses, although businesswomen still tend to find the time. There is a tendency among many Australian fathers, perhaps unconsciously, to leave the disciplining and nurture of the children to their mother, even when the mother is in the work force. It does change if the couple have actually planned a role-reversal or have applied egalitarian principles to the care of their children.

At a time when drug abuse and suicide are on the rise amongst youth, this situation is even more critical. The distance between many young people and their parents was captured poignantly for me in a television comedy I saw some years ago where Dad has just come home from work; he takes a stubby from the fridge and sits down to watch the news. His son bursts in though the front door and starts racing up the stairs. Dad calls out to him, 'Hi son, how's your adolescence going?' This may be comic exaggeration, but it makes the point — indeed, is not far from the truth — in too many cases.

I have recently made the decision of going to my son's basketball match at least once a fortnight. The return trip takes me just over an hour, yet the connections we are both making are invaluable. He is thirteen years old, but in what will seem like five minutes time, he'll be asking for the keys to the car and then moving away from home. I'll never get these years back again in spite of my busy schedule. I still have time to make some changes, thank God.

We can be cut off not only from our children, but sometimes also from our wider family and friends as we allow the intensity of life to consume us.

I thank God also that three years before my mother died I decided to put a line through my diary one night a month to go and have an evening meal with her. Of course, my whole family saw her regularly on various occasions, but those mother and son nights were so special — Mum in her mid seventies, me in my early forties. Even when she became too ill to cook, she would insist on me getting Chinese takeaway and paying me for it when I arrived. The meal didn't really matter. The space was sacred.

All this is uncomplicated equipment for the journey of a good marriage and family life. There is obviously much more that could be offered and I recommend the professional agencies and resources listed at the back of this book.

Putting together our skills, plans and goals, we are really saying three very profound words in action: *I love you*. It is time to move on to examine all that true love means as the foundation to our lives.

I LOVE YOU

I love you,
Not only for what you are,
But for what I am when I am with you.

I love you,
Not only for what you have made of yourself,
But what you are making of me.

I love you,
For passing over all my foolish and weak traits,
That you can't help but see.

I love you,
For drawing out into the light my beauty
That no-one else had looked quite far enough to find.

I love you.

Author unknown

6

Understand the ingredients of love

MANY PEOPLE GET CONFUSED WHEN THEY TALK seriously about love because the word can mean so many things.

We only have the one word in English; in New Testament Greek there are four! Consequently, you can love your work, a child can love her pet rabbit, you can love to go on a picnic, you can love your friends or relatives, you can love life and people in general, you can be 'in love' with someone, and you can 'make love'.

The majority of us would agree, however, that in whatever form it takes and expresses itself, love is *the* most important thing in life — the only really sacred thing, the one thing that cannot be questioned. If real love dictates your action then it must be okay.

In the fifth century, St Augustine said *Dilige et quod vis fac*[1] — 'Love and do what you will' — and there was nothing new about that. The Old Testament prophets and Christ himself said much the same long before when talking about the first great commandment.

The only new thing reflected in some modern values and standards today is that many people leave out Augustine's first word! 'Do your own thing' was a popular phrase a few years ago. Remember the bumper sticker: 'If it feels good, do it'? A nice recipe for social disaster!

Be that as it may, love is undoubtedly still the rage today, though considerably cheapened in many areas of life. We read about it, hear songs about it, see movies about it, tell jokes about it. Yet there are people who will never know love in its true fullness at all.

I had a sixteen-year-old girl in my office recently who thought that the word 'love' was meaningless. She had 'made love' to a lad whose second name she didn't even know.

✠ Love of others is a reflection of God's love for us

What has Christianity to say about this slippery word 'love'? Primarily, it states that 'God is love and those who abide in love abide in God, and God abides in them' (I John 4, verse 16). God's love comes first. 'In this is love, not that we loved God, but that he loved us. . .' (I John 4, verse 10). The most perfect gift of his love is Jesus Christ, whose sacrificial love is the example for all human love: '[God] sent his son to be the atoning sacrifice for our sins. Beloved, since God loved us so much, we also ought to love one another' (I John 4, verses 10 and 11). All human love, therefore, derives from God's love.

Jesus himself said:

> *I give you a new commandment, that you love one another. Just as I have loved you, you also should love one another. By this everyone will know that you are my disciples if you have love one for another. . . As the Father loved me, so I have loved you; abide in my love. If you keep my commandments, you will abide in my love, just as I have kept my Father's commandments and abide in his love. I have said these things to you so that my joy may be in you, and that your joy may be complete.*[2]

St Paul helps to unpack the qualities of love in his first letter to the Corinthians:

> *Love is patient; love is kind; love is not envious or boastful or arrogant or rude. It does not insist on its own way; it is not irritable or resentful; it does not rejoice in wrongdoing, but rejoices in the truth. It bears all things, believes all things, hopes all things, endures all things.*[3]

So, human love doesn't mean physical or psychological conquest of another person where the other is seen only as a thing, as an object who merely becomes one more trophy on the mantelpiece of our desires. Jesus loved and accepted people for themselves and their lives, in his light, were released to be more truly God's re-creations. We will explore this more fully in chapters 7 and 8.

If our love is to be a reflection of the way God loves us, we must find our relationships with others releasing them to be more truly human. I mentioned earlier that particularly in marriage, we are to be partners who complete each other's being, delighting in the love we share. Someone once put it that in a good marriage, the joys are doubled because there are two to celebrate and the problems are halved because there are two to carry the burden. God delights in us when he beholds us loving in this way! For we are created for love.

In the film, *Chariots of Fire*, I remember the Scottish runner, a devout Presbyterian, saying: 'When I run, I feel his pleasure!' In the sport of human love, we are right to feel God's pleasure.

This awakening to divine love has done amazing things to people, even some who choose the celibate life. Thomas Merton, a Trappist monk who died in 1968, lived in the strictest of monastic conditions in a hermitage in Kentucky, USA. Yet he would speak of such inner growth and a festive sense of God's presence in words that remind me of the way I felt after my first date with the woman who is now my wife: 'Love sails me around the house. . . I walk two steps on the ground and four steps in the air. It is love. It is consolation. . . to say that I am made in the image of God is to say that love is the reason for my existence, for God is love.'[4]

This was a far cry from the days of his English schooling where any spiritual growth was killed by a chaplain for whom the word 'gentleman' was more appealing than 'love'. Verse 1 of the famous I Corinthians 13, once modified, was an often-repeated text for services: 'If I talk with the tongues of men and of angels, and be not a gentleman, I become as sounding brass.' Sadly, the 'God is a stiff upper lip Englishman' mentality, like its Aussie Ocker counterpart, is still with us, as mentioned earlier in connection with pride. This thinking stifles the gift and flow of genuine love.

Elsewhere, Merton says: 'Love is the key to the meaning of life. It is at the same time transformation in Christ and the discovery of Christ. As we grow in love and unity with those who are loved by Christ. . . we become more and more capable of apprehending and obscurely grasping something of the tremendous reality of Christ in the world, Christ in ourselves and Christ in our fellow. . .'[5]

Our greatest dignity, the essence and most intimate secret of our humanity, is our capacity to love.

Gabrielle Bossis in her dialogue with God as recorded in her book, *He and I*, reveals a most innocent and profound communion with divine love:

> *The Father says: 'You are astonished by my love. There is only one explanation: God's extravagance. So just believe in all simplicity in this love of an all-powerful being. . .*

And give yourself up to his infinitely delicate and tender omnipotence. Be taken captive by love and ask for grace. Love me with my love and be full of trust. . .

'Practise the presence of my love. I am everywhere. Put your head on my heart. Of course, since this pleases me. If you only understood the gift of God and who it is speaking to you. . . Come to me, then, and bring others in your heart. . . fan flames of your love. . . don't stand still. Never cease to go forward. Enter ever deeper and deeper into my heart. Reading about my passion is not enough. Make it part of your very self. Wherever you are, take my sufferings. Sufferings desired, willed, expected. . . they are my love for my children — for you.'[6]

We do need to remember that in real life, *true* love is often born of passion, pain, suffering or misunderstanding. In any worthwhile relationship, this will be discovered as we are refined in love. It was so with God's greatest gift of love in Christ. It cost him. True love is vulnerable. St Paul reflects on this cost:

. . .we have peace with God through our Lord Jesus Christ, through whom we have obtained access to this grace in which we stand; and we boast in our hope of sharing the glory of God. And not only that, but we also boast in our sufferings, knowing that suffering produces endurance, and endurance produces character, and character produces hope, and hope does not disappoint us, because God's love has been poured into our hearts through the Holy Spirit that has been given to us.[7]

✠ The qualities of God's love that speak to human relationships

What are the particular ingredients, then, in the love of God that can speak so strongly to our human relationships? I believe that there are four main ingredients: love is a personal decision; love is a searching pursuit; love is a satisfying commitment; love is a sacrificial vocation.

❒ *Love is a personal decision*

The personal love of God was manifested right at the beginning of creation. His very act of bringing all life into being, and especially our lives 'in his own image' was an intensely personal, self-giving offering of love. But the most perfect and complete sign of God's personal love was in the offering of his own beloved son to our world to redeem us and transform our lives, reflected in one of the best-known texts in the Bible, John 3, verse 16: 'For God so loved the world that he gave his only Son, so that everyone who believes in him may not perish but may have eternal life.'

Someone said, 'God so loved the world that he didn't send a committee!' and we can certainly be grateful for that for, in this context of personal encounter, there is a huge difference. You can't have love in an impersonal, calculated boardroom arrangement.

The love of God is intimate. This intimacy is revealed so clearly in Jesus. His life is like a beautiful stained glass window through which God's love shines. God looks for us in the person of Jesus Christ and says: 'Here. . . this is my love for you. . . my gift of abundant life for you. . . will you receive it?'

The relationship between Jesus and the Father is the secret to the personal love of God and a key for our lives and our own relationships. In his conversations with the Father, Jesus used the word 'Abba' which literally means 'Dad'. In fact, when the disciples asked Jesus, 'Teach us to pray,' he said, 'When you pray, say "Abba — Father, hallowed be your name. . ."' Our prayer lives are, therefore, meant to be more personal than pious, walking in conversation with one hand in 'Dad's' as we tell him about our day and our desires.

I know someone who felt God to be so distant in his spiritual life up until one special day in the Holy Land. He was sitting by the Sea of Galilee at a place well-trodden by Christ when he noticed a little boy running along the shore. The boy stumbled over a rock and grazed his knee. He then went running to his father in tears, crying 'Abba! Abba!. . .' His father took him up in his arms to comfort him and reassure him. My friend burst into tears, too — tears of joy. At last, he had a personal, intimate image of God. Alleluia!

I cannot help but wonder, in passing, if this is one reason that many men in particular find it hard to develop that ability to 'let go and let God' work in their lives. Is it that they never had that relationship with their earthly dad, let alone our heavenly Father?

The scriptures make it abundantly clear that this intimate relationship is something for all of us, because of God's personal gift of love in Jesus:

> *When the fullness of time had come, God sent his Son, born of a woman, born under the law, so that we might receive adoption as children. And because you are children, God has sent the Spirit of his Son into our hearts, crying 'Abba! Father!'* [8]
>
> *When we cry 'Abba! Father!' it is that very Spirit bearing witness with our spirit that we are children of God and, if children, then heirs, heirs of God and joint heirs with Christ.'* [9]

The 'Abba' imagery may, however, not be helpful for the reader if there has been a difficult relationship with one's own father since childhood. If this is so, then simply change it to 'Mum' or some other image that works. For example, I once had a woman with me in spiritual direction who had a miserable life with both parents. She was very fond of music, particularly symphonies. She found the symbol of 'conductor' quite appealing in developing a personal prayer life. God now calls her tune and directs her music beautifully! Of course, he always has.

As we see a personal relationship with God develop in prayerful conversation so, with our human relationships, mutual discourse is a natural beginning. We must take positive steps to get to know each other. In fact, in one part of France where two young people start courting, they are said to be 'talking to each other'. Here, a simple local custom has a wisdom that goes right to the heart of love.

True love begins with the personal decision to get to know someone — and this knowledge comes through conversation. It is this profound truth that makes me most uneasy about people who put the sexual cart before the horse like that young girl in my office who had 'made love' with someone whose second name was not known to her. There was no real love to make because there was no real personal knowledge; indeed, the 'knowledge' was only carnal.

In a relationship, this journey of knowledge must never end, particularly in marriage, for marriage is a 'lifelong union in which a man and a woman are called so to give themselves in body, mind and spirit, and so to respond, that from their union will grow a deepening *knowledge* and love of each other'.[10]

Therefore, this personal decision of love must involve a continual and deliberate process of searching and discovery. Sadly, too many relationships have failed when people have either thought they knew everything about each other, or just stopped talking. The decision to pursue love actively had been abandoned.

❐ *Love is a searching pursuit*

One very popular image of Christ is that of the good Shepherd. A favourite psalm for many people is Psalm 23: 'The Lord is my shepherd.' The intimacy of the biblical symbolism can, however, be lost on some who are used to huge sheep stations where there is infrequent contact between shepherd and sheep — and that, sometimes, by helicopter.

Things were on a much smaller scale in biblical times — and still are in much of the Holy Land today. The shepherd often literally knew the sheep 'by name' (John 10, verse 3) and would seek out the ones that were lost or hurting or threatened by wolves and weather. He would get to know them and their peculiar habits individually.

In such a way we are called, in love, to seek each other out. To say that 'love is blind' is nonsense. Infatuation may be blind, but love is searching. Someone who truly loves wants to know the object of his or her affection through and through, warts and all. That is how Christ feels about us — he is there watching for us constantly, looking out for us particularly when we stray, wanting to bring us home to the fold. What does that say about our human relationships?

How do you seek out your lover when he or she strays from you? Do you make the first move, even if you're feeling wounded, to reconcile, or do you leave your lover in the wilderness to 'learn a lesson'? You may have to wait a long time. As God in his Shepherd-Son brings us back into communion with him, so must we also seek to restore loving communion with each other.

On a more positive note, the true joy of love as a searching pursuit is in discovering more and more beautiful things about our partner. I have been married for twenty years and I am still finding out lots of information about my partner. Explaining and sharing each other's feelings is a good way to continue growing in knowledge of each other. There are still plenty of surprises waiting for us around the corner, most of them hopefully pleasant ones! If you haven't had any lately, perhaps you're taking your relationship for granted, or you're no longer searching — or no longer expecting to discover anything new. It's never too late to take up the journey again.

Sometimes in our relationships, one of us is in need of direction and advice. The shepherd love of Christ is a helpful image in this regard as well. In the Christian faith, we can find a steady guiding light. Christ's direction is sure: 'He leads me in right paths for his name's sake' (Psalm 23, verse 3). He increases hope and conviction, rather like the leader out front in the old television Western, *Wagon Train*.

You can't help admiring the strength of will and purpose that he manages to inject into a mixed-up and essentially incompatible bunch of people on that convoy he's leading to their destination. He gets them there by sheer will-power, by strength of personality — giving them energy, courage, inspiration and determination to reach their promised land.

You and I are meant in our relationships to be like that for each other, especially in those moments where we might feel we have lost our way, or lack the energy to go on. We can be so strong for each other at these times, learning to 'carry' one another as Christ has carried us. We can often forget he's right there with us, our 'other partner' in life.

Some years ago I wrote a reflection about this:

BY MY SIDE

'When in doubt, panic.' A friend said that to me once when I was in need of some sound advice and made me laugh at myself. He could see that I was *in a panic!*

Ever had one of those days when nothing seems to go right; when the world seems to be having a go at you?

Most of the times I find myself in these panic situations are when I've got up in the morning and gone like a bull at a gate, looking only to my own resources, and then wonder why I fall flat on my face. I create my own storm in a teacup and, if my panic spreads, then my whole family is tossed around in the storm as well. I've left something, someone, out.

Lord, you are there all the time, but I don't always notice you and I panic. You must laugh at me sometimes, or cry, at my little faith. Give me the serenity and quiet confidence that comes from knowing that you are always there by my side.[11]

❒ *Love is a satisfying commitment*

In John's Gospel, in the very same chapter about the good shepherd (chapter 10), Jesus says, 'I came that they may have life, and have it abundantly.' God's gift of love in Jesus offers us a satisfaction beyond description.

We touched on that briefly in the writings of Thomas Merton and Gabrielle Bossis. Abundant satisfaction is what we need in a world with its fleeting changes and chances. When two people are in love, they are competely taken up with each other, they completely satisfy each other. Our human love is meant to be the kind of satisfying commitment to each other that Christ has towards us. God's plan in Christ is to gather up all things in one great celebration of love.

The Bible paints a picture of extravagant delight!

Blessed be the God and Father of our Lord Jesus Christ, who has blessed us in Christ with every spiritual blessing in the heavenly places, just as he chose us in Christ before the foundation of the world to be holy and blameless before him in love. He destined us for adoption as his children through Jesus Christ, according to the good pleasure of his

> *will, to the praise of his glorious grace that he freely bestowed on us in the Beloved.*
>
> *In him, we have redemption through his blood, the forgiveness of our trespasses, according to the riches of his grace that he lavished on us. With all wisdom and insight he has made known to us the mystery of his will, according to his good pleasure that he set forth in Christ, as a plan for the fullness of time, to gather up all things in him, things in heaven and things on earth.*[12]

There are some beautiful words in that reading that we can take into our love lives, too. May our relationships be ones filled with good pleasure, lavishing each other with riches and blessings, that our love might be gathered up in God's love.

The Greek word for the love mentioned in this reading is *agapé*. It implies a disposition, a temperament — an attitude of heart, mind and will that is deep and abiding, not superficial, fleeting or fancy. It is the same love that Paul describes in I Corinthians 13. In the teaching of Christ, it is a set determination to serve the highest interests and needs of the one we love. Sometimes, our selfishness can get in the way of this, but this is our goal, our aim and, because it is meant to be two-way traffic, it is completely and utterly satisfying.

We are called to be passionate lovers in imitation of this *agapé*-love. Love must be freely taken and freely given in a gay abandonment of delight and self-giving.

Such love goes beyond the way the world tends to think of love. So much of the love we hear about today is conditional and laced with ulterior motives. This is especially and paradoxically so in the lives of those who are given to us often as role models in glossy magazines — their marriages frequently fail because what has been left out all too often from the very start is probably the most important ingredient of all: sacrifice.

❒ *Love is a sacrificial vocation*

Again, the image of Christ the Shepherd speaks powerfully to this fourth ingredient: 'The good shepherd lays down his life for the sheep.'[13] He is the true shepherd because he lays down his life. His sacrifice is part of his office. When we say, 'God so loved the world that he gave his only Son. . .', we are talking about a cross, for that is where Jesus had to go to gain eternal life for us. This is the most costly and vulnerable part of true love, but love loses its authenticity without it.

The sacrifice that love demands is the secret ingredient in any healthy relationship and particularly a marriage. It is the sacrificial element in love that distinguishes it from mere lust or even goodness. Lust is 'in it for me'. Love is 'in it for you'. Lust grasps at things and people in momentary fashion. Love gives and gives and never counts the cost — indeed, achieves complete satisfaction through giving.

A tutor of mine once said that the true test of love — when you really love someone — is the preparedness to give that person up if it will mean his or her complete happiness. This — perhaps at first glance strange — litmus test can be applied not only to mismatches in the stormy world of love before marriage, but also to extramarital affairs that may sometimes involve genuine love but, if pursued, will cause tremendous harm to a lot of people.

In similar fashion, for our happiness and ultimately for our salvation, God gave up his Son. For Jesus, every deed, every word, every thought was for others. There isn't a trace of selfishness to be found anywhere in his character. Upon the cross, he laid down his life for us. How much do we lay down of ourselves in our love for others?

The cross itself is a tremendous symbol for married love. St Paul said: 'May I never boast of anything except the cross of our Lord Jesus Christ, by which the world has been crucified to me and I to the world.'[14] In a good marriage, the husband and wife are called to nail to the cross those things that will prevent them from truly being the partner God has intended each one to be. When in the marriage service the officiant says, 'Will you give her/him the honour due to her/him as your wife/husband and, *forsaking all others*, love and protect her/him as long as you both shall live?',[15] that is exactly what is intended.

In one sense, it is a costly, sacrificial statement. Sadly, too many marriages have failed because very little is *forsaken* by one or both parties. The marriage service has always acknowledged that there will be problems and difficulties in marriage, but how quickly in many cases do couples forget the very realistic and sacrificial words they say: 'For better for *worse*, for richer for *poorer*, in *sickness* and in health.'

These traditional words are far from sentimental — they go to the core of the married condition as experienced by most people. It is a condition to be confidently embraced, not opted out of. It is the sacrificial nature of true love that challenges us all to really hang in there with those we love. This quality will be explored in more depth in the next chapter.

Sacrificial love also has an implication for our relationships with society as a whole and the wider world. How different does the other man, woman or child look when viewed through such loving eyes — even the most difficult people with whom we find so many differences or hang-ups. They are often God's way of giving us another point of view in life, past our own often blinkered vision.

Such love breaks down barriers and produces abundant fruit because it sees such amazing possibilities. This is not the way many people love. This is a different, greater kind of love — a love that goes far beyond what is expected, far beyond the normal decent thing to do.

An art critic who beholds and studies a painting can understand more about it than a novice. She discovers harmony, emotion, meaning and life between the colours and the features. Through this experience, the art critic goes beyond an ordinary person in her reaction and response as well.

The lover who receives a card or flower from the beloved sees beyond the paper or the petals which are mere symbols to the love which is symbolised and, in so doing, is drawn in deeper union to the beloved. This is a very sacramental thing.

Where many might only see the surface of things — and there is a great deal of superficial living going on today — all of us are called to probe deeper and find their true inner dimension. It is there that we discover the meaning of life and the purpose of our existence. It is there that we discover the Divine Lover, whom we call God.

When they had finished breakfast, Jesus said to Simon Peter, 'Simon, son of John, do you love me more than these?' He said to him, 'Yes, Lord, you know that I love you.' Jesus said to him, 'Feed my lambs.'

A second time he said to him, 'Simon, son of John, do you love me?' He said to him, 'Yes, Lord: you know that I love you.' Jesus said to him, 'Tend my sheep.'

He said to him the third time, 'Simon, son of John, do you love me?' Peter felt hurt because he said to him the third time, 'Do you love me?' And he said to him, 'Lord, you know everything; you know that I love you.'

Jesus said to him, 'Feed my sheep. Very truly I tell you, when you were younger, you used to fasten your own belt and to go wherever you wished. But when you grow old, you will stretch out your hands and someone else will fasten a belt around you and take you where you do not wish to go.' (He said this to indicate the kind of death by which he would glorify God.) After this he said to him, 'Follow me.'

John 21, verses 15 to 19

7

Love by hanging in there, whatever

'DO YOU LOVE ME?' HOW MANY times in history do you think that question has been asked?

Wives sometimes ask their husbands that question: 'Do you love me?' 'Of course, I love you; I work for you, don't I? — I buy you presents!' Husbands sometimes ask the same question: 'Do you love me?' In the film, *Fiddler on the Roof*, the wife says: 'For forty years I've mended your clothes, cleaned your house, cooked your food, slept in your bed — how can you ask, do I love you!' Modern egalitarian living hasn't changed the scenario much, either.

This question is often asked after something hurtful occurs — or has been said — or an action hasn't been forthcoming that may have been expected and disappointment follows.

A boyfriend and a girlfriend go to a party. The girl spends most of her time appearing to chat up other boys. Later, the boy asks her, 'How could you do that to me? Don't you like me any more?'

Parents have children with discipline problems at school or at home. Perhaps their child has been stealing. They look at each other and ask, 'Where did we go wrong?' They may be tempted to say to the child in a fit of anxiety, 'Don't you love us any more?'

Scripture records this question being asked three times in a row: 'Do you love me?' The questioner is Jesus. I believe that this particular portion of scripture contains the most vital truth about love that we can ever know: the joy of reconciliation through genuine forgiveness.

I like to call this 'hanging-in-there love'. This story about Jesus and Peter right at the end of John's Gospel is offered here as a model, not only for our marriages, but also for other important relationships, including those in business life. It has three key elements. Hanging-in-there love means that you:

* forgive in full knowledge that you have been rejected
* are prepared to make the first move
* reassure the other that he or she is loved.

✠ Forgive in full knowledge that you have been rejected

Near the end of 1981, my wife and I visited Coventry Cathedral in England. It is an impressive modern cathedral that rises, phoenix-like, beside the ruins of the old cathedral destroyed by German bombs in the World War II. I was very impressed by the decor and acoustics of the new cathedral with its famous sculpture of Michael and the devil fixed to the outside wall. But the most moving thing of all was to be found in the ruins of the old cathedral.

There, it is still possible to see where the altar once stood and beneath that place are inscribed two words still left after the bombing, words which bear testimony to what Christian faith and love are all about: 'Father, forgive.'

These are the words that the dying Jesus spoke from

the cross. They were spoken for those who were crucifying him, mocking him, abusing him. They were putting God's love made flesh to death. And this incarnate love, even at the moment of extreme agony and dying, continued to love them. Knowing full well their actions, Christ could only offer back amazing love. Most of us will never have our love tested to anywhere near this extreme.

On the way to the cross, all the disciples had forsaken Jesus and fled, including Peter. Peter had originally protested that even if all the other disciples forsook Jesus, he wouldn't. He went so far as to tell Jesus: 'I will lay down my life for you.' But Jesus answered him, 'Will you lay down your life for me? Very truly, I tell you, before the cock crows, you will have denied me three times.'[1]

Peter followed Jesus after his arrest to his place of trial, but this was as far as he went. For at this place, when questioned about his knowledge of Jesus and as his Master had predicted, Peter denied him three times. When the crunch came, to save his own skin, Peter disowned Jesus. Most of us will not experience in our own relationships such a vehement denial — an action leaving us isolated and vulnerable as Jesus was at that moment. It is little wonder that when Jesus looked upon Peter, Peter 'went out and wept bitterly'.[2]

Each of the four Gospels records this threefold denial in vivid detail; it is only the Gospel of John that records the threefold reinstatement of Peter by Jesus, thereby giving us the total picture.

Three times Jesus asked Peter, 'Do you love me?' The Gospel of John records that the third time Jesus asked this question, 'Peter felt hurt' and then he said to Jesus, 'Lord, you know everything; you know that I love you.'

Many years ago, I caught a bus into the city and some very special words were printed on the ticket: 'A friend is someone who knows everything about you and likes you just the same.' That is ultimately how God feels about humanity. He is the one 'to whom all hearts are open, all desires known and from whom no secrets are hidden'[3] — and who loves us just the same.

The words of Peter and those words on the bus ticket truly expose the *unconditional* nature of true love, and of genuine forgiveness. Peter didn't *deserve* Christ's love; Jesus just freely gave it to him and, in doing so, released Peter to be the great Christian saint that God had always wanted him to be. Clearly, this saint was a sinner, but a forgiven sinner whom Jesus reinstated in the full knowledge of what he had done.

You often hear the expression 'forgive and forget'. I think it's full of holes! True forgiveness involves the free and complete acceptance of a person in love, knowing full well that they have offended, albeit never again holding this sin against them. But we never forget it. Indeed, our love often grows in strength, joy and confidence as a consequence of it. You can believe Peter's did. There is another related expression people sometimes use. When one person apologises, sometimes the other person says, 'O, forget it.' That can be a put down. It can also imply that you do not honour the person's need to say they are sorry. They don't want to forget it — they want to be forgiven. There is a huge difference.

Much of the world is not tuned in to this unconditional 'hanging-in-there' love. I meet people all the time where the bottom line in the way they talk and live is obviously:

'I'll love you if you keep your job.'
'I'll love you as long as I can be independent.'
'I'll love you unless you're nasty to me.'
'I'll love you unless you hurt me.'

The actual words may not be said. But when the crunch comes and the going gets tough, the weak back off. Yet God doesn't love us *only if* we are kind to each other. God doesn't love us only if we keep his commandments or only if we say our prayers and stay out of trouble. He loves us, period! — with no strings. His desire is for us to do all the above and more, but not in order to earn his love or a place in his kingdom, but as a response to his unconditional love. True repentance is always a response to love, not a condition placed on love. It is because he hangs in there with us even when we stray that we have the glorious opportunity to say, 'Sorry, Lord, I goofed that time!' And he says to us, 'Okay, I forgive you. Let's start again' — and off we go with a clean slate.

There is a beautiful story in scripture popularly known as 'The Parable of the Prodigal Son'. It has something very pertinent to say about hanging-in-there love. More accurately, it is the parable of the loving father. It describes how a man had two sons. One of them took his share of the inheritance and went off and squandered all of it in loose living. He sees the error of his ways and decides to go back to his father in the spirit of repentance. On his way home, 'while he was still far off, his father saw him and was filled with compassion; he ran and put his arms around him and kissed him'. It is a parable about human repentance and God's abundant forgiveness.[4] And the most glorious thing about it is that he is even more willing to forgive us than we are sometimes to repent.

The Anglican Church has a magnificent prayer at the end of the service of Holy Communion that captures this miracle of reconciling love:

Father of all, we give you thanks and praise
that, when we were still far off,
you met us in your Son and brought us home.

Dying and living, he declared your love,
gave us grace and opened the gate of glory.
May we who share Christ's body live his risen life;
we who drink his cup bring life to others;
we whom the Spirit lights give light to the world.
Keep us in this hope that we have grasped;
so we and all your children shall be free,
and the whole earth live to praise your name.[5]

This quality of God's meeting us when we are still far off leads to the second element of hanging-in-there love.

✠ Be prepared to make the first move

When we are hurt or offended by our loved one, we can feel naturally inclined to retreat and lick our wounds and wait for that person to come to us, apologise and make amends. That may seem like the logical thing to do. Certainly, as I observe the popular media and counsel many people experiencing breakdown, that attitude is well entrenched. An 'eye for an eye, tooth for a tooth' Old Testament-retribution view of life is still alive and well in many relationships as well as in corporate business and international dealings.

The great problem with stand-off tactics is that the person who causes the offence may not sort it out by such tactics. He may be unaware that the other is hurting; she may be too humiliated to come and sort it out; he may be completely ashamed now that resentment has set in; or, she may actually feel justified in having created the division. We can often sit in a corner waiting for an apology that may never come or an act of reassurance that will never occur.

I suspect that Peter was humiliated and ashamed by his denial of Jesus and convinced that Jesus would have nothing to do with him again. After Christ's resurrection, there is no record of an apology by Peter. Instead, there is this amazing account in the Gospel of John of Christ making the first move.

The setting is the conclusion of breakfast by the Sea of Tiberias. The disciples, including Peter, had just been fishing and the risen Jesus became known to them in a huge catch and in the act of sharing in the bread and in the fish. When they had finished breakfast, we might have expected Peter to sidle up to Jesus saying, 'Lord, can you possibly forgive me for what I have done to you?' But it is Jesus, the betrayed one, the denied one, who makes the first move to Peter and says, 'Do you love me?'

Of course Jesus, in doing this, took the risk of being put down again. That is always the risk we take when we make the first move, but it is a risk well worth taking. For if we don't, we may never know the joy of the reconciliation that will almost certainly unfold like the caterpillar into a beautiful butterfly.

Imagine the expression on Peter's face when Jesus began this renegotiation: 'Simon, son of John, do you love me?' I see Peter looking at Jesus first almost in disbelief, thinking, 'You want to know if I love you after what I have done? I should be asking *you* this question, Lord.' But it is Jesus asking the question and thereby opening the door for Peter to come in and say, 'Of course I love you; I always have.' Jesus knew the heart of humanity[7] and he certainly knew Peter better than Peter knew himself. Even when he 'looked on' Peter in the act of denial, Jesus knew the real Peter, the true potential — he knew that Peter would come home reconciled in love and ready to catch more than fish.

But Jesus had to make the first move.

I believe that there is no greater secret in a relationship of love than this. This is the key that unlocks the impasse that so many marriages get into and breaks another pathetic 'rule' mentioned in the first chapter — namely, 'concentrate on your rights and privileges'. This impasse was touched on in the earlier chapter on pride. Even so-called friends can become our enemies at this point in a marriage, because they will often encourage us not to give in, to stick to our guns or go for the jugular and reinforce the negative vibes we have about our partner instead of the positive.

Soapies on television encourage this attitude, too. I'm told that people don't take them seriously, but I'm not convinced. If you watch and listen to bad teaching and bad living long enough, you end up believing it.

The Bible says: 'Love does not insist on its own way.'[6] There is no room for negotiation at all if I convince myself that, because I am the one who has been wronged, my partner is therefore entirely responsible for putting things right again. This position is the direct antithesis of the Christian gospel and is a death-dealing blow to marriage. Peter and many other great biblical characters would have been good only for the garbage heap if this principle had been applied to them. Sadly, thousands of marriages have failed for this very reason.

The reader may want to make some space to ask the question: 'Is there an impasse in my relationship where I have been hurt or misunderstood, but where I perhaps need to make the first move?' However hard it may be, it is a move worth making.

✠ Reassure the other that he or she is loved

We should never take it for granted that our partners know that we love them. Jesus had to know from Peter's lips as well as in his life that he loved him. Even though he knew what was in Peter's heart, he still had to hear it. (I often tell people that is why we should pray. God may know what's on our minds, but he delights in hearing from us!)

Peter needed the same assurance from Jesus. Jesus doesn't actually say the words to Peter. His very act of reconciliation was love-in-action. But he also drives it home by giving Peter a threefold commission: 'Okay, you love me — then here's what I want you to do: feed my lambs. . . tend my sheep. . . feed my sheep. . . follow me.' Peter knew that he was back in the good books because he was also given a responsibility as a sign of his reinstatement. A great responsibility indeed, for his pastoral and missionary work would end up costing him a price — the same supreme sacrifice paid by his Master and Lord. Yes, Peter would indeed 'lay down his life' for Christ — there was just this hiccup in the middle!

Sometimes in our human relationships, our forgiveness may only be half-hearted because, while we may have said we still love our partner, we may become reluctant to let our loved one hold the reins again. He or she perceives that while we have said, 'All is forgiven', we don't mean it. Jesus certainly took another big risk in handing the reins to Peter, but that is what true forgiveness is all about. In the full knowledge of what has happened, there is not only the total offering of love, but also the empowering grace and freedom given to move onto the task at hand. It may be that yet another moment of weakness lies ahead, but often the sense of release and joy is so great in forgiveness that we become much stronger in character and faithfulness.

Reassurance must be in word and in deed. When did you last say to your partner, 'I love you', and also back up your claim with a sign as Jesus did to Peter when he said 'feed my sheep'? It may just mean happily handing over those keys again when the car returns from the panel-beaters or really sounding relaxed when the phone rings and — guess what? — 'I'm caught up at the office, darling. . .'

The scribes and the Pharisees brought a woman who had been caught in adultery: and, making her stand before all of them, they said to him, 'Teacher, this woman was caught in the very act of committing adultery. Now in the law Moses commanded us to stone such a woman. Now what do you say?' They said this to test him, so that they might have some charge to bring against him. Jesus bent down and wrote with his finger on the ground.

When they kept on questioning him, he straightened up and said to them, 'Let anyone among you who is without sin be the first to throw a stone at her.' And once again he bent down and wrote on the ground.

When they heard it, they went away, one by one, beginning with the elders; and Jesus was left alone with the woman standing before him. Jesus straightened up and said to her, 'Woman, where are they? Has no-one condemned you?'

She said, 'No-one, sir.' And Jesus said, 'Neither do I condemn you. Go your way, and from now on do not sin again.'

John 8, verses 3 to 11

When Jesus saw the crowds, he had compassion for them, because they were harassed and helpless, like sheep without a shepherd.

Matthew 9, verse 36

8

Love, despite failure

MARRIAGE PROBLEMS AND SEXUAL SINS figure quite prominently in the Bible and often among prominent people! King David in the Old Testament and Mary Magdalene in the New are two who readily come to mind.

The story of David's adultery with Bathsheba is found in 2 Samuel chapter 11. This affair is particularly sinister. When David discovers Bathsheba is pregnant, he sends for her husband Uriah who is in battle to come home, encouraging him to sleep with his wife so as to make it appear that the baby is his. When Uriah refuses to do so as an act of loyalty to David and his fellow warriors, David then has him sent to the front line in order that he will be killed. Following Uriah's death and Bathsheba's time of mourning, David then marries her.

David's sin becomes known to the prophet Nathan who exposes it before him, proclaiming that the sword would never depart from his house because of this evil. David confesses his sin and Nathan pronounces God's forgiveness saying, 'Nevertheless. . . the child that is born to you shall die.'[1]

In this episode, David would learn of the mercy of God in forgiving him the sins of adultery and effectively of murder. He could also learn compassion, for while not entering into Bathsheba's grief for her husband, his grief in the loss of their child was intense.[2]

Adultery, while still forbidden in the Ten Commandments, does not carry with it the penalties of biblical times. It isn't even grounds for divorce in Australia any more.

I remember the newspaper columns when I was a teenager that laid before the eyes of the reading public those who were filing for divorce, often because of adultery. In those days, people would hire private detectives to literally catch people 'in the act'. My friends and I used to giggle as we read the columns, but I stopped laughing one day when my best friend found his mother's name listed as a co-respondent. That *wasn't* funny. We were both horrified!

The Gospel of John records that the law of Moses commanded stoning to death as a penalty for adultery and, typical of the patriarchal society, it is a woman who cops it. It doesn't say anything about the bloke![3] What is important in this encounter with Jesus, as in another encounter we will examine shortly, is that the focus shifts from the sin to the sinner. No-one, including Jesus, denies the sin. It is sin all right. But Jesus takes it so much further than some of his religious critics were prepared to go.

What was the background to this act of adultery? We don't know. But one thing we can perceive as we look at this tragic scene is that adultery is almost always a *symptom* and not a cause of something going wrong. In this woman's case, I suspect that she had never known a meaningful relationship of love, that perhaps she was a victim of circumstances beyond her control.

All sin is an attempt to blot God out of his creation — to act as though he were not there. This is particularly true of sexual sin. The late Dr John Gaden had some very helpful words to say in connection with sin, grace and the redemption of sexuality:

It is a distinctively Christian viewpoint to hold that every created reality is finite and fallen as well as being good. Our sexuality, God-given as it is, can neither solve all our human problems nor escape the contamination of sin. At the same time, because it is from God, it has the potential for being redeemed and becoming redemptive.

Sin has to do with our alienation from God, our turning and being turned from the right orientation of our life toward God and our neighbours. Sin distorts all our relationships, including that with our self.

We may make sexuality our God, and direct all our energies to serving the goal of more and more sex. We may treat marriage as a licence to abuse our partner sexually. We may be so obsessed by sexual fantasies, both negative and positive, that we are unable to develop a real relationship with other people of either sex. In each case, our sexuality has become destructive of our self. Unrestrained desire and feelings of revulsion are both sins against sexuality, being unfaithful to oneself and God. This lack of fidelity is perhaps the deeper meaning of porneia *(loosely translated as 'immorality') and its connection with idolatry.*

In the service of God, our sexuality will be creative and redemptive, an expression of our chastity, fidelity and integrity. By being drawn into a sexual relationship with another person in which our individuality is respected, we learn the worth of our body-selves as sexual beings and the vulnerability required of intimate giving and receiving. Being accepted, loved deeply and forgiven by another raises us from self-doubt and provides the stability necessary for personal growth. Being able to make a commitment to others and having a self from which to reach out to them requires a self-acceptance and self-affirmation that must include loving our own bodies and our sexuality.

Yet we cannot do that unless we know that we are already loved. The gracious unconditional love of God, which is the context of our being, is often mediated to us first through the love of others — parents, friends, lovers, givers of pastoral care.[4]

There is a little saying in church circles that needs to be taken more seriously, particularly by the church itself. It goes: 'Hate the sin, but love the sinner.' If Bible heroes like David, Peter, Paul — who called himself the 'chief of sinners' — and others, including this woman, could be set free truly to become what they were created to be, then there are bound to be thousands of ordinary men, women and children around today who need to know this liberty, too.

✠ A modern story of failure and compassion

Greg and Lindy were one such couple whom I had the privilege of counselling over a sustained period of nearly three years. The original stumbling block was Greg's adultery.

On two actual occasions, Greg had slept with a woman who worked at his business. Prior to this, she had offered Greg a listening ear and had come across as a sensitive, caring person. It was at a time when his marriage was in a fairly typical state of mutual, albeit unconscious indifference. Things looked good on the surface and the children were quite happy and settled in the home environment. Lindy was very involved in her professional life which Greg found threatening, especially because Lindy earned more than he. She often worked longer hours and their social life was virtually non-existent.

Greg informed Lindy of his brief affair as a way of shocking her into some kind of change. Lindy was devastated. She immediately ordered him out of the house as she began to come to terms with his admission. However, from that day and for the next thirty months, the family continued to live under the one roof 'for the sake of the children', but the environment was strained and often hostile.

Greg promised Lindy that these few moments of

weakness would never happen again. They were over — he still loved her. But Lindy's verbal attacks upon him became more and more abusive, the children often going to their bedrooms in tears because of the tension.

Both Greg and Lindy started seeing me separately for counselling very soon after Greg's confession. Lindy refused to come with Greg, so this was the next best thing. They came individually for over two years.

The agenda for Greg was usually focused on survival. He wanted to stay in the marriage. He still loved Lindy. Paradoxically, she was coming home earlier — mainly, it seemed, to prove to the children that she was very committed to them in the situation. He thought that, if things got better, they could use this time to their advantage, but right now he felt 'worse than what the cat dragged in': Lindy's treatment of him had the effect of making him feel totally soiled and disgraced, before her and God, with no hope of a fresh start.

Lindy's agenda mainly focused on her inability to forgive Greg. He had violated their marriage. She said she had just as much reason to have had an affair as he, but would never have dreamt of adultery. Greg was 'gutless'. Her anger revealed an even deeper feeling: her hurt and humiliation. We dealt with that at much length and over many months.

The first breakthrough for both of them occurred not long after Lindy began to feel less immediate pain whenever we spoke of Greg's unfaithfulness. Both he and she began to acknowledge, from different angles, that their marriage had been far from satisfactory for many years and that they had become distant from each other, just going through the motions. Neither of them could remember when they had last sat down and talked together about their relationship and plans for the future. Too much was being taken for granted.

Greg recognised that he had failed to initiate any opportunities to get out of the rut they were in. Lindy felt she had become too preoccupied only with the needs of the children.

Slowly, Lindy began to see for herself that Greg's unfaithfulness had been a symptom rather than a cause of breakdown in the relationship. She certainly knew that their sex-life had been sporadic and far from inspiring. Greg, for his part, often admitted in sessions together that he hadn't affirmed Lindy for her achievements, particularly in her career, and that he was sure it had had a detrimental effect upon their physical relationship.

The next and most wonderful breakthrough occurred in the final of many sessions on forgiveness with Lindy. She realised that her subsequent treatment of Greg, at this stage for well over two years, had been far *worse* than his original two isolated acts of adultery. To use the analogy of John chapter 8, the weight of stones she had thrown at Greg for over two years far exceeded the weight of Greg's sin.

To cut the rest of this long but fruitful story short, we all had a magnificent family reconciliation together sitting on their lounge room floor where I had the joy of laying hands on them both, and their children, pronouncing God's forgiveness and healing. Greg, like the prodigal, was finally met by Lindy who, while hurt, would no longer condemn. She could see her sin, too. No more stones, just tears of joy. He became truly the person she knew everything about and loved him just the same!

In fact, as things turned out, they began at that moment the marriage they were always meant to have. But that is hardly surprising. From that point, they became wonderfully open to each other: partners who could complete each other's beings, while still fully prepared for the occasional tiff!

✠ An ancient story of failure and compassion

The importance of loving acceptance, compassion and forgiveness as being the prerequisites for healing and fullness of life is made clear by this account:

One of the Pharisees asked Jesus to eat with him, and he went into the Pharisee's house and took his place at the table. And a woman in the city who was a sinner, having learned that he was eating in the Pharisee's house, brought an alabaster jar of ointment. She stood behind him at his feet, weeping, and began to bathe his feet with her tears and to dry them with her hair. Then, she continued kissing his feet and anointing them with the ointment.

Now when the Pharisee who had invited him saw it, he said to himself, 'If this man were a prophet, he would have known who and what kind of woman this is who is touching him — that she is a sinner.'

Jesus spoke up and said to him, 'Simon, I have something to say to you.'

'Teacher,' he replied, 'speak.'

'A certain creditor had two debtors; one owed five hundred denarii and the other fifty. When they could not pay, he cancelled the debts for both of them. Now which of them will love him more?'

Simon answered, 'I suppose the one for whom he cancelled the greater debt.'

And Jesus said to him, 'You have judged rightly.' Then turning toward the woman, he said to Simon, 'Do you see this woman? I entered your house; you gave me no water for my feet, but she has bathed my feet with her tears and dried them with her hair. You gave me no kiss, but from the time I came in she has not stopped kissing my feet. You did not anoint my head with oil, but she has anointed my feet with ointment.

'Therefore, I tell you, her sins, which were many, have been forgiven; hence, she has shown great love. But the one to whom little is forgiven, loves little.' Then he said to her,

'Your sins are forgiven.'

But those who were at the table with him began to say among themselves, 'Who is this that even forgives sins?'

And he said to the woman, 'Your faith has saved you; go in peace.'[5]

A lot of social rules are broken both by the woman and Jesus in this encounter. When we look at the themes of pride, shame, forgiveness, wholeness and freedom, there is a manifest difference between the woman and Simon, the host of the dinner. No doubt a number of guests were surprised to see who ended up feeling free and who ended up being bound.

Simon certainly got more than he bargained for when he asked Jesus to eat with him. I like to think that he also went on to recognise his own need for forgiveness and that he came to love others in a powerful way.

But look at this woman. Previously, no-one else had understood her, or accepted her for *herself* (not her body) or wanted to know about her. No-one, that is, until now — a man who somehow made you feel your worst in his company and yet, at the very same time, your best. She certainly had made many mistakes and committed many sins. But he forgave her. No-one else had — not the religious people, probably not her family — but this man did. There was no need to condemn her — she knew her condition. But he seemed to get to the root of the matter, the 'dis-ease'. He understood, he accepted, he saw her for herself — a whole woman. And it made her a new woman, a new creation.

Psychologists say that as many as sixty per cent of their patients would find healing if they could find forgiveness and, in particular, if they could forgive themselves. This is no doubt another serious factor in the reasons for low self-esteem mentioned in the chapter on loving yourself unconditionally.

Christ wants to bring out the best in all of us, as he did in this story — that is the reason for his coming and is the essence of his nature. I think that we are often more hard on ourselves than he would be in his rich compassion.

✠ The role of respect and compassion in marriage failure and divorce

It is the compassion of Christ that is particularly appealing in respect to marriage failure and divorce. The church has taken what has seemed to many to be light years to catch up with this aspect, which is so obviously apparent in any faithful reading of the New Testament. It is the same Christ who says, 'What God has joined together, let no-one separate' who also says, 'Let anyone among you who is without sin be the first to throw a stone.'[6]

It is the same Paul who says that 'the husband should not divorce his wife' who also says, 'If anyone is in Christ there is a new creation: everything old has passed away; see, everything has become new.'[7] The woman in Simon the Pharisee's house would certainly have agreed with Paul!

Happily, this new understanding, blending Christ-like discipline with Christ-like compassion, has meant that people who have had the trauma of breakdown, separation and divorce have been able to start afresh. The Anglican Church, for example, has in many places changed its rigid position on this matter in the last twenty years. Once there was no hope of marriage for a divorced person in the church; now there is every hope, particularly for those who truly encounter the newness of life that Christ offers.

The road of marriage is not an easy one. It involves human beings who make mistakes. While we should never deny that the estate of marriage is a lifelong union only to end in the death of one or the other partner, it must be clearly recognised that some marriages die long before either partner does. The trauma of an irretrievably broken-down marriage is hard enough on the people concerned without others failing to exercise the ministry of Christ-like compassion, understanding and respect, thereby adding to the burden.

Respect and compassion are two very undervalued qualities in today's world — and more's the pity for it. They can transform our closest domestic relationships and reshape the course of nations, for these qualities acknowledge the supreme worth and value of every human being.

Someone for whom we have a never-failing respect and admiration is someone we can trust — the sort of person who will never let you down. Fundamentally, our partner in marriage should be such a person — indeed, our best friend. But it goes much further than this. Christ seemed to have an amazing quality of respect for a great number of people, particularly those who had little respect for themselves — the poor, the diseased, the downcast, the disappointed, the grieving. In contrast, he had little respect for the 'respectable' people.

We are called to take Christ-like respect and compassion into all our human dealings and at many levels. We have already seen how Jesus broke many social rules in his desire to touch people at their real point of felt need — he went so far as to wash his disciples' feet when some of us might hesitate even to polish another person's shoes.

All the people mentioned in this chapter — David, Greg and Lindy, Simon the Pharisee, this grieving woman and others — had one underlying, first and foremost need: the need to be loved. Dr Jack Dominian, the Senior Consultant Psychiatrist at the Central Middlesex Hospital in England, often uses a phrase in his lectures: 'the blissful certainty of being wanted'. [8] This is our most basic, if sometimes unconscious, desire. It is with us from the womb. It is meant to be totally affirmed in early childhood and, where it isn't, the consequences can be quite harmful.

My own childhood was lived in mostly material and financial hardship. Yet I can honestly say that both my parents overwhelmingly gave me the blissful certainty of being wanted. I told that to my mother just before she died in the Christmas of 1991. It was a possession beyond price. It is never too late for us to offer this gift to others, be they our closest relations or the neighbours we are called to love as we love ourselves.

When I was on a clergy retreat in 1990, the leader was the chaplain to the Perth Children's Hospital, Father Doug Davies. He spoke of God's mercy and forgiveness in terms of 'cuddling'. When we have fallen and are hurting, God wants to give each of us a warm cuddle. He is 'slow to chide and swift to bless'.[9]

Doug's experience in hospitals has heightened this awareness. He spent a lot of time at his hospital cuddling children, parents — and nurses. (He said he was old enough to cuddle nurses!) There were often very sick children, anxious parents and emotion-charged nurses. It doesn't matter, in this respect, how ill the child is: this kind of contact means more than physical health itself. It provides the blissful certainty of being wanted, of being loved, and that is the most important thing in life or death.

Authentic compassion and respect is founded upon this common human need. This is why Jesus, when he saw the crowd, ministered individually to them, one by one; hands-on, touching, forgiving, healing, restoring, in his deep compassion.

Mother Teresa of Calcutta in her ministry to millions was heard to say: 'I never see the crowd. If I saw only the crowd, I would never get started. I minister to the individual.'

No doubt the reader knows one or two individuals who would benefit immensely by this kind of personal attention: perhaps someone in grief, hurting from a divorce, or a lonely person? Why not reach out to them in this way? Christ has no hands but ours, as the following reflection suggests:

> *Loneliness is the smell of gas and last year's calendar hanging on the wall. If you've been to many old boarding houses or apartment blocks, you'd know what I mean. That's where the lonely people live, and there's probably one or two in your street as well.*
>
> *I can't think of anything worse than loneliness. I'd rather be in pain with someone there to hold my hand, than to have every material benefit and no-one to talk to.*
>
> *Jesus experienced extreme loneliness, those times when it seemed that the world had forsaken him, when no-one understood his mission. And the world still forsakes him in my lonely brother and my lonely sister. Inasmuch as I have done nothing for them, I have done nothing for him.*
>
> *Lord, help me to be so very sensitive to the needs of the lonely and the afflicted of your world, my world. Can I really worship you in word and sacrament if I do not tend to you in my needy brother and sister? Help me to worship you and find you there, too, Lord.*
>
> *Bless those who seek out the lonely people, and thank you for each one who finds hope and a purpose for life again.*[10]

There was a wedding in Cana of Galilee, and the mother of Jesus was there. Jesus and his disciples had also been invited to the wedding. When the wine gave out, the mother of Jesus said to him, 'They have no wine'. . . Now standing there were six stone water jars for the Jewish rites of purification, each holding twenty or thirty gallons.

Jesus said to them, 'Fill the jars with water.' And they filled them up to the brim. He said to them, 'Now draw some out and take it to the chief steward.' So they took it. When the steward tasted the water that had become wine and did not know where it came from (though the servants who had drawn the water knew), the steward called the bridegroom and said to him, 'Everyone serves the good wine first and then the inferior wine, after the guests have become drunk. But you have kept the good wine until now.'

John 2, verses 1 to 3, 6 to 10

9

Love in a spirit of adventurous celebration

THERE'S NO STANDING STILL in the celebration of life and love. We are here to be surprised by joy!

When I was on long-service leave in 1988, my family and I went to Uluru (Ayers Rock) in the centre of Australia. The Uluru climb is not your average family outing. At the base there is a sign, warning of the dangers to those with heart ailments, fear of heights and the other health or fitness problems.

I have a fear of heights. I had gone less than halfway up the chain by which one hauls oneself up the first part of the climb when I had to stop. But not for breath or rest — we were all quite fit, having walked for miles around Kakadu National Park, checking out the wetlands and Aboriginal rock paintings just a few days beforehand. No, this was fear. I *froze*!

I asked my eight-year-old son if he wanted to keep going. I was afraid for him, too. He said, 'Yes.' I was hoping for 'No'!

But when I reached the top, I had a feeling of such exhilaration, joy and achievement. Standing there with William, looking at the amazing panorama before us, was an opportunity for praise and wonder at creation. It was a heady experience! It felt good to be alive, to be there, to have strived, to have accomplished.

I'm sure that much of this could be said about marriage. Sometimes we may not want to take the risk of moving in our relationships because we are afraid. Change can be a frightening thing. But unless, with God's strength, we do summon up the prayer and nerve to keep going, we may well miss out on the true joys and the magnificent new horizons that are awaiting us beyond our imagination.

It would seem all too easy, sometimes, in marriage to pull out when things look a bit threatening. But some of our greatest moments of love and joy await us on the other side when the obstacles are overcome.

I certainly know that if it were not for the persistence of my small son William, I would never have completed the Ayers Rock climb. There is another 'still small voice'[1] calling us ever upward to new heights if we would listen. This wind of change may speak to us in a variety of ways and often in the most unlikely of places, but with it there is always a festive sense of celebration.

✠ An ancient story of marriage celebration

One such place was a wedding in Cana of Galilee which Jesus attended (John 2). The most notorious thing about this wedding reception is that the wine ran out. That's just about as disastrous as a pub with no beer! This became the setting for Jesus' first miracle or sign.

He changed water into wine. And not just a small glassful, not a bottleful, not even a bucketful but, according to my maths, about 650 litres of the stuff. Not only that, but it was top quality, full-bodied wine, better than what had already been drunk — the steward who had the first sip said so! What does all this mean, especially in the context of marriage?

One marriage rite says: 'Christ adorned and beautified matrimony with his presence and with the first sign by which he revealed his glory, at the marriage in Cana of Galilee; and holy scripture commands that all should hold it in honour.'[2] Well, that's providing that you can still stand up straight! With miracles like this, one can't help feeling relieved that they couldn't drive home. But fancy Christ permitting such abandoned merriment. All this wine — hardly the respectable thing to do. Loaves and fishes would have been much more in keeping.

No, the two things we just can't avoid in this story are that Christ brings change and he also brings laughter and joy. He's here to liven up the party and, if we find that strange or even distasteful, it might be that we've got the wrong religion. For this is just a foretaste of even better things to come in the great Wedding Banquet being prepared for us at the close of the age.

The change is certainly one of astounding quality. The jars of water were for the Jewish rites of purification. They represented the old order of things — a ritual that had to be repeated over and over again. Jesus tells his mother that his 'hour is not yet come', which might seem a strange thing to say at a wedding. But he is referring to his own ritual of purification to be accomplished once for all upon the cross.

The wedding at Cana was the first manifestation of his glory. The cross was his supreme moment of glory. This would bring about the greatest purification and transformation in history — of sin and death into eternal life.

Christ's presence in a marriage can have a similar purifying and transforming effect. Our thoughts, desires and actions can become more other-centred rather than self-centred as we fix our eyes on his presence and celebrate with him as the head of this house, the unseen guest, the silent listener. . . Praying together in his presence further enhances this quality of 'otherness'. The life of Christ is the greatest ingredient to life after the wedding. You never know what might happen next. Cana tells us this and much more.

A wedding is always a joyful occasion. Everyone is caught up in the love of the bride and groom and they express this in a variety of ways. Delightful and often extremely humorous stories are told about the couple and their respective parents. People want to laugh because it is an occasion to express that often stifled side of our humanity. Life can be too serious. Religion can be too serious and there is nothing worse than a 'stuffy' wedding! Cana tells us it doesn't have to be this way.

People get quite light-hearted at weddings; sentimentality rises to an all-time high — and many, though perhaps tearful, are supremely happy. Something good and right is taking place and most are determined to enjoy it to the full. They joke, they remember, they laugh, they eat and drink — and, one has to confess, some drink a lot. This truth is freely admitted in the Cana story.

So one can't help feeling that as well as showing us a change in the order and quality of things, Christ had likened his presence in our lives to the merriment of a wedding. Where he is present, there must be life, light, laughter and joy. And if there isn't, he may just have some heady surprises waiting for us — by the bucketful.

✠ How to make our marriage a time of celebration

It is important to make a regular examination of our relationships to find the cobwebs, the stale air, the poor wine, and ask some straightforward questions. You can dialogue together about these:

When did we last have a good belly-laugh together?
What is my idea of fun these days?
Do we play together?

When did we last do something quite idiotic?
Is life mainly ordinary and predictable?
What new books have I read?
What new people have I met?

(Og Mandino maintains that the only things that make us different in five years' time to what we are now are the people we meet and the books we read.)[3]

What family celebrations have occurred lately?
When did we last have a good vacation?
Why do I want to stay in your life?
I need you now especially for. . .
What is the happiest thing that's happened to us in the last year?
Am I feeling fulfilled right now? If not, why not?
Do we have some worthwhile plans and goals?
Is our sex life special or just routine?
Are the children happy and enjoying home, school, etc.?
Are we spending enough quality time with the children?
Do the children think we are happy?
When did we last have a 'naughty weekend' away?
When did we last renew our marriage vows? *(See Appendix B.)*
What about a Marriage Enrichment or Marriage Encounter weekend? *(See Appendix A.)*

It might be good to pray together about some of the things you share. Then, allow Christ to blow away the cobwebs with his breath of life and pour in new wine. Celebrate! These are your salad days!

Change is a sign of growth. The only way to tell that a tree is healthy is to observe the changes: new branches, new buds, new blossoms — and fruit. It is a sign that the tree is alive and purposeful. The same is true of a marriage or any worthwhile relationship. A marriage that doesn't change, doesn't grow and blossom, or bears no fruit (and here I don't mean children) is a dead marriage.

Jesus told a parable about a fig tree not bearing fruit. In the story, the gardener suggests that he could dig around it and put manure on it. This is precisely what we do in marriage when we sit down together and dialogue about what is working and what needs improving or changing. I often use the expression, 'What you see is what you get.' Fruit-bearing in marriage depends on our vision. What do you 'see' for your marriage?

I often make a seemingly strange statement to couples preparing for marriage. 'Each morning when you wake up, always see someone you still need to get to know.' By that I mean that there is always something more to discover about my partner. He or she is not my own flesh and blood (like our children). We can always find new dreams and hopes together, never taking each other for granted.

Sometimes, I think we compromise our human nature and our capacity to reach new heights. When Christ died on the cross, rose and ascended into heaven, he took with him our vulnerable human nature — redeemed by the gift of his life to this earth. Yet we often make excuses about our human nature.

I hear people say: 'Well, I'm only human, after all.' But Jesus took this nature that we might be *completely* human! We can no longer despise or excuse our humanity, nor apologise for it. It is what God chose to assume when his Word became flesh — that we mortals might become as he is. By receiving Christ and living repentant lives, it is our privilege and joy to claim the power to be the children of God.

Sadly, how much in the history of humankind has our nature sunk to deeds of shame. People have perpetrated crimes against humanity too horrible to contemplate, have allowed millions to starve, have encouraged moral and political corruption on a massive scale. Yet there is another aspect to our humanity — a wholesome and attractive quality. There would be very few people on this planet who do not know of the simple goodness of human nature, of human sacrifice and care, of human joy and fulfilment, of human courage and endurance, of human warmth and kindness. We also know that the mighty have fallen in recent times as a consequence of extortion, fraud and corruption — they, too, have that potential and shouldn't be written off.

All of it, the good with the bad, Christ has taken in his redeeming love and, in doing so, has shown us that our human nature is so utterly capable of the highest nobility, praise and beauty.

And all this, in fact, gives the full perspective to our everyday lives as we queue in the rain for our bus, get the kids off to school in the morning, answer that difficult letter, cope with our sick child, or watch a loved one dying.

In our married and family life, we are given this power to ascend to new heights — to be, in reality, the people we are meant to be in God's plan. In many ways, it is like learning to become a child again, for children don't usually take life as seriously as adults and we are all children of God.

Jesus said: 'Truly I tell you, unless you change and become like children, you will never enter the kingdom of heaven.' [4] The reason Jesus said this was that children acknowledge their dependence upon their parents, particularly little children. Similarly, we all need to acknowledge our dependence on God. Scripture even encourages us to become like newborn babies.

I vividly remember all my three children when they were babies and particularly their bonding to Deborah through breast-feeding. Newborn babies are so dependent on their mothers: for their care, their warmth, their milk.

I wrote a reflection about William not long after he was born. Part of it goes:

> *Little William looks so content at his mother's breast. Yes, he longs for that food — many an anxious cry is quickly abated as he clamps onto that food supply. When he's hungry, no amount of backpatting or hugs or smiles will do the trick; there's only one thing on that young mind.*
>
> *I should long for your resources like that, Lord — quelling my false anxiety and preserving me from self-righteousness. How often your word says we have to be more like babes and children. . . I can see why.*
>
> *Thank you, Lord, for William and for every new birth. Help me to be born anew by reaching for the food of your Spirit, craving for it, until I am satisfied by nothing else.*[5]

I encourage the reader to take a look with the mind's eye at the children in the family, if there are any. Looking back to one's own childhood is a worthwhile exercise, too — rediscover the child that is still within you! You will find something intensely liberating, something that you're not meant to let go of in riper years. Tell your children never to let go of it, either. Not childishness, but childlikeness. Adults can be so calculating, ulterior, serious and absurdly unadventurous! Certainly, get wisdom, get insight, plan, decide, but be open to your dreams, your awe, your wonder, your inspiration — so many amazing possibilities.

In 1991, I took the funeral of a man who had died in the middle of life and who left behind a son aged sixteen. I was reminded of my own father who died when I was seventeen, at the age of fifty-four: too young. But this man apparently had taken life a bit too seriously and had now lost his opportunity to change that — in this life, anyway.

His son read the following reflection, believing that the

words could easily have flowed from his dead father's lips:

> *If I could live my life over again, I'd make more mistakes. I would relax. I would limber up. I would be sillier and crazier than I have been, this trip. I would take very few things seriously; I'd laugh more and cry less. I wouldn't worry about what other people thought of me. I would accept myself as I am. I would climb more mountains, swim more rivers and watch more sunsets. I would eat more ice-cream and less beans. I would have more picnics and watch less TV. I would feel only sad, not depressed; concerned, not anxious; annoyed, not angry. I would regret my mistakes, but not feel guilty about them.*
>
> *I would tell more people that I liked them. I would hug my friends. I would forgive others for being human and hold no grudges. I would play with more children and listen to more old people. I would go after what I wanted without believing I needed it, and place less value on money.*
>
> *You see, I am one of those people who live cautiously and sensibly and sanely, hour after hour, day after day. Oh, I've had my moments — and if I had my time over again, I'd have more of them. In fact, I'd have nothing else: just moments, one after another, instead of living so many years ahead of each day. I have been one of those people who never goes anywhere without a thermometer, a gargle, a hot-water bottle, a raincoat and a parachute. If I could do it over again, I would do things and go places and travel lighter. I would plant more seeds and express my feelings without fear.*
>
> *I would start barefoot earlier in the Spring and stay that way till later in the Autumn. I would play hooky more: I wouldn't get such good marks, except by accident. I would ride more merry-go-rounds. I'd pick more daisies and smile more, because I'd be living free.*[6]

It's time to drink the new wine, ascend to new heights, rediscover our childhood and be free!

Jesus said to his disciples, 'In my Father's house there are many dwelling places. If it were not so, would I have told you that I go to prepare a place for you? And if I go and prepare a place for you, I will come again and will take you to myself, so that where I am, there you may be also.'

John 14, verses 2 and 3

10

Love to the end

I AM ONLY FORTY-SIX. MY WIFE IS STILL on the downside of forty, but we are already talking about our retirement! It's because we really enjoy going places and just doing things as a couple — that's how our marriage began and that's how it's going to finish before one of us falls off the perch.

We thoroughly enjoy each other's company and look forward to the time where there's just the two of us again, albeit hopefully with lots of grandchildren within driving distance.

If there is life after the wedding, then there has to be life after children, too. I feel terribly sad for couples who divorce after the children have all left home, but I can understand why it happens. I know a couple who, just after their twenty-fifth wedding anniversary, in the prime of their life and still years before retirement, split up. They said they no longer had anything in common, which is a tragedy, but their parting was amicable. Unknown to all except their closest friends, they had been drifting apart for years, but delayed their departure until all the children had left the nest.

Jack Dominian says of this empty-nest stage: 'Some parents have lived only through their children and when they depart there is not only a deep sense of loss, but the couple look at each other and see a stranger. It often happens that each partner has derived their meaning from the relationship with their children. They have lived, eaten and made love with each other, but the significant element of the marriage has been the children. So when they go, there is little left to the relationship. This has been particularly true of earlier cohorts of marriage, which emphasised exclusively the importance of marriage in terms of family rather than as an interpersonal relationship.'[1]

It is this interpersonal relationship that needs to be kept alive and well between the partners themselves all the way through the marriage. In the marriage service, we are asked to give due honour to our partner and, *forsaking all others,* love and protect each other as long as we both shall live.[2]

I happen to entertain the perhaps radical belief that the word 'forsaking' even includes children. That doesn't mean my wife and I forsake them — we spoil them rotten and love them to pieces! What it does mean is that we put each other's love and protection first, knowing and trusting that everything else, including the children who are the extensions of that love, will be provided for. Our children certainly didn't ask to be born and we have to give them the best possible love and upbringing we can, but they are a gift only on loan.

We must always, however, be able to look at our partner and say proudly within our hearts if not out loud, 'Here is my greatest asset.' Then, long after the children have left home and the grandchildren start appearing, the two of us will continue to grow and blossom in the halcyon years of our love.

So, along with all the planning and goal-setting mentioned earlier, it is a great idea to talk over the latter years of marriage and certainly the retirement years. At the time of writing, the big issue on nearly everyone's lips is superannuation. The newspapers are full of advertisements about it — television commercials abound on the subject: 'planning your nest egg'.

Having financial and material security in the later years is important, but having a lot in common, a sense of deep companionship, and more wonderful dreams to fulfil — that is more important. I can't help feeling that there is too much concentration on the former and that some couples are therefore left with a rather hollow, albeit comfortable existence in retirement.

Some of the things you may like to discuss are:

What will be our main interests and hobbies?
What new interest could we consider together? Fishing? Golf? Gardening?
What friends will be significant? Who are those who might even travel occasionally with us?
Where do we want to go? What do we want to see? (Be honest about places you don't think you'll have time to see until you retire — then you can look forward to that time.)
What projects might we complete or commence?
What parts of our career lives will still influence us?
Will our church life be more or less involved?
What about other organisations?
How will we structure time for our children/grandchildren?
Will we be fully or only semi-retired?
Do we want to order the greater part of each year and map out actual holiday times, or just live from day to day and be more spontaneous about decisions?
Are our wills in order?
Have we planned for our funerals?

Planning for your funeral makes a lot of sense. Appendix C at the back of this book contains a list of details that will make things so much easier for your family, clergy and the funeral director when the time comes.

Even after a long period of illness, one can never really be prepared for the death of a loved one. There is no 'right' time to die in the sense that it will always be accompanied by feelings of shock, bewilderment, emptiness. . . I often encounter bereaved spouses or relatives who are too bewildered to have to sit down and plan a funeral, or think about what their loved one would have liked to be done and said.

To have your plans written down beforehand with copies in the possession of next of kin, clergy and funeral director can considerably relieve this burden. Most funeral companies are highly reputable, but I have to admit that in my experience some grief situations have been exploited by financial charges above and beyond what was necessary, with numbed relatives allowing the funeral director to 'just see to it, please'. This, too, can be avoided by planning beforehand with the more objective clear-thinking that goes with it.

As Appendix C suggests, pre-paid funerals make a lot of sense, too. They can involve considerable saving as well as giving peace of mind in time of loss. I thoroughly recommend making a time to talk to both clergy and the funeral director of your choice to arrange all these things.

Having all things in order like this again says three very simple but profound words: I love you. It means that you care enough for those who are left behind that they needn't worry about the nuts and bolts. Indeed, by doing this you will release them to embrace their grief more fully and have the space to deal with it more creatively.

In this connection, I once had a very sad situation involving a woman who had been single all her life and an extremely committed, practising Christian. In fact, her church family was in many ways her only family. She hardly ever missed a Sunday and was very involved in her church's social and welfare life as well. The holy communion service was her life-blood.

When she died, the first I knew of it was through a phone call from the funeral director. His instruction was that her next of kin, a nephew and businessman in the eastern states, on a tight schedule, was flying to Perth for a quick private cremation and would I conduct it?

That wasn't a problem. What was a great concern was the fact that her church family was cut off from this experience — indeed, the service would not even take place in her spiritual home. Certainly, we still had a memorial service for her a few days later, but it was not the same. All this could have been avoided if her clear wishes had been put down on paper, including what I am positive would have been a desire for the Holy Eucharist and joyful hymns of resurrection.

I therefore encourage readers, particularly practising believers, to make the time to do this. It needs to be remembered that those given the responsibility of making the arrangements may not be practising worshippers themselves, so if you feel a church funeral is important, beat them to it!

There is another very important question for us to ask each other. It might be too sensitive and difficult for some, but I believe it is another beautiful way of caring even beyond the grave. The question is: 'What will you do when I die?' I find it hard to contemplate a time when either my wife Deborah or I will be separated in this way from each other. But this fact is as certain as life itself.

Dealing with the loss of a lifelong partner in marriage must be one of the hardest challenges in life. I minister to many people trying to adjust to it. They often admit that the very person they want to share their loss and pain with is the one they've lost. But it takes me no closer to what I think my own pain would feel like with such a loss.

My late mother lived as a widow for nearly the same amount of time that she had been married — around twenty-five years. She often said, 'Women have an amazing ability simply to potter. Men don't know what to do with themselves.' In my experience, her observation was quite close to the mark. Certainly, I am sure that this is the reason why more widowers marry again than do widows. Men are much more dependent than the macho-image would dare admit!

Just to be able to share how we feel about each other's death will be something we can reflect back upon when the time comes. We might want to make a few promises to each other: 'Now don't you stop going out in the boat. . . pruning the roses. . . cooking the roast. . . writing me love letters. . . just because I'm not here.'

There is a beautiful little statement that I often share at funerals that captures how we might feel about each other when our final breath is over:

TOGETHERNESS

Death is nothing at all — I have only slipped away into the next room. Whatever we were to each, that we are still. Call me by my old familiar name; speak to me in the easy way which you always used. Laugh as we always laughed at the little jokes we enjoyed together.

Play, smile, think of me, pray for me. Let my name be the household word that it always was. Let it be spoken without effort. Life means all that it ever meant. It is the same as it ever was; there is absolutely unbroken continuity. Why should I be out of your mind because I am out of your sight? I am but waiting for you, for an interval, somewhere very near just around the corner.

> *All is well. Nothing is past; nothing is lost. One brief moment and all will be as it was before — only better, infinitely happier and for ever. We will all be one together with Christ.*[3]

I have written a letter to each member of my family to be read in the event of my death. I really recommend this idea, too. It can be a source of tremendous assurance and comfort in time of loss, and so much warmer than just leaving a will.

The great joy for the Christian is that there is life after life! *Resurrection* life. Upon another shore and in a greater light, Jesus tells us we 'neither marry nor are given in marriage, but are like angels in heaven'.[4]

In the meantime. . . may you, the reader, accept the joyful challenges of the homework of marriage. Build upon the foundations of your love-nest an impenetrable fortress to withstand the false values around you. May your marriage be filled with all the richness this beautiful world has to offer.

And may God go with you to strengthen, enfold and bless.

Postscript

Love is in the air! Who could be more sure of that than the one who knows, experiences and shares the joy of unconditional love with another?

The Christian gospel is an invitation to fall in love. Indeed, Christianity has often been described as 'the School of Love'. It is the setting of God's love affair with this world. God is in love with us and wants us to love him in return, along with those who are created in the image of his love: the people with whom we live and work and share our being.

There are so many similarities between the way that God loves us and the way we are meant to love each other, particularly in marriage. Jesus said, 'Those who love me will keep my word, and my Father will love them, and we will come to them and make our home with them.'[1] When you love someone very much, you want that person to stay with you. One of the first things I said to my wife before I officially proposed to her was, 'I want to be with you and live with you for the rest of my life.'

I used to find it very hard to go home sometimes after going out to dinner together or going to a movie; I wanted it to last forever! I can remember doing crazy things like driving right across Adelaide to see her after a meeting at 10.30 at night instead of going home to bed. I'd tap on her bedroom window and she would come out and sit in the car for a couple of hours. We had many more late nights when courting than we do now. But in marriage it is so good to be under the same roof together — to *make our home* together. God's love in Jesus Christ wants to have a home with us, too; in fact, his love is the secret to authentic married love.

When a young man presents the girl he loves with a little parcel, beautifully wrapped and tied, he hopes that she will open it in his coy anticipation and, when she finds the diamond ring inside, that she will place it on her finger as a sign that their love is mutually committed with a view to a lifelong relationship. She is saying to this offering, in token of his love, 'I love you back.'

The Bible refers to Christ as the bridegroom and to the church (meaning the Christian community) as his bride. In a similar way to the public character of marriage, we are called to wear his love for all the world to see.

Sadly, for many people, God's love in Christ remains unrequited, still wrapped up as it were and left upon the dressing table as other pursuits distract and consume. But he remains faithfully in love and waits, like a loving parent looking out for a wayward child, yearning for us to come home.

There is only one kind of security worth having and that is the abiding love of the God who makes his home with us — for this is heaven.

Appendix A:

Approved organisations offering programs of marriage counselling and marriage education

New South Wales

Anglican Counselling Centre, Sydney
HEAD OFFICE
56 Bland Street
ASHFIELD, NSW 2131
Phone: (02) 9799 9311

Life Care Counselling and Family Services
20 Glassop Street
BANKSTOWN, NSW 2200
Phone: (02) 9708 2088

Centacare, Catholic Community Services
HEAD OFFICE
6th Floor, Polding House
276 Pitt Street
SYDNEY, NSW 2000
Phone: (02) 9283 3099

Family Life Movement of Australia
HEAD OFFICE
16 Jersey Road
STRATHFIELD, NSW 2135
Phone: (02) 9747 3988

Relationships Australia
HEAD OFFICE
5 Sera Street
LANE COVE, NSW 2066
Phone: (02) 9418 8800

UNIFAM
(The Marriage and Family Counselling Service of the Uniting Church)
HEAD OFFICE
4th Floor
262 Pitt Street
SYDNEY NSW 2000
Phone: (02) 9261 4077

Christian Psychological Services (Aust) Pty Ltd
PO Box 640
MONA VALE NSW 2103
Phone: (02) 9997 1565

Westside Counselling Centre
7 Wandana Avenue
BAULKHAM HILLS, NSW 2153
Phone: (02) 9639 0949

Salvation Army Counselling Service
93 Queen Street
NORTH STRATHFIELD, NSW 2137
Phone: (02) 9743 2831

VICTORIA

The Anglican Marriage Education and Counselling Service
HEAD OFFICE
Level 5
227 Collins Street
MELBOURNE, VIC 3000
Phone: (03) 9654 7360

The Cairnmillar Institute
HEAD OFFICE
993 Burke Road
CAMBERWELL, VIC 3132
Phone: (03) 9813 3400

Catholic Family Welfare Bureau
HEAD OFFICE
396 Albert Street
EAST MELBOURNE, VIC 3002
Phone: (03) 9662 2033

Family Relationships Institute
HEAD OFFICE
21 Bell Street
COBURG, VIC 3058
Phone: (03) 9354 8854

Relationships Australia Victoria
HEAD OFFICE
Suite 307
1 Princess Street
KEW, VIC 3101
Phone: (03) 9205 9570

QUEENSLAND

Anglican Family Care
HEAD OFFICE
Webber House
439 Ann Street
BRISBANE, QLD 4000
Phone: (07) 3839 1333

Centacare, Catholic Family Services
HEAD OFFICE
Morgan Street
FORTITUDE VALLEY, QLD 4006
Phone: (07) 3252 4371, 3252 4373

Relationships Australia
Queensland
HEAD OFFICE
159 St Paul's Terrace
SPRING HILL, QLD 4000
Phone: (07) 3831 2005

AUSTRALIAN CAPITAL TERRITORY

Relationships Australia
Canberra and Region Inc.
HEAD OFFICE
15 Napier Close
DEAKIN, ACT 2600
Phone: (02) 6281 3600 (after 18 August 1997)

Centacare, Catholic Community Services
PO Box 3167
MANUKA , ACT 2603
Phone: (02) 6239 7700 (after 18 August 1997)

SOUTH AUSTRALIA

Adelaide Central Mission
HEAD OFFICE
1st Floor, Mission House
10 Pitt Street
ADELAIDE, SA 5000
Phone: (08) 8212 2599

Anglican Community Services
HEAD OFFICE
18 King William Road
NORTH ADELAIDE, SA 5006
Phone: (08) 8239 8200

Centacare Catholic Family Services
HEAD OFFICE
33 Wakefield Street
ADELAIDE, SA 5000
Phone: (08) 8210 8200

COPE
HEAD OFFICE
116 Hutt Street
ADELAIDE, SA 5000
Phone: (08) 8223 3433

Relationships Australia
South Australia
HEAD OFFICE
55 Hutt Street
ADELAIDE, SA 5000
Phone: (08) 8223 4566

WESTERN AUSTRALIA

Anglican Marriage and Family Counselling Services
HEAD OFFICE
Ground Floor, Geoffrey Sambell Centre
42 Colin Street
WEST PERTH, WA 6005
Phone: (08) 9321 5801 (after 5 May 1997)

Catholic Marriage Preparation and Education Centre
HEAD OFFICE
459 Hay Street
PERTH, WA 6000
Phone: (08) 9325 1859 (after 5 May 1997)

Centrecare Marriage and Family Service
HEAD OFFICE
456 Hay Street
PERTH, WA 6000
Phone: (08) 9325 6644 (after 5 May 1997)

Relationships Australia
Western Australia
HEAD OFFICE
755 Albany Highway
EAST VICTORIA PARK, WA 6101
Phone: (08) 9470 5109 (after 5 May 1997)

Wesley Central Mission
HEAD OFFICE
Marriage Education Department
2nd Floor, Wesley Centre
93 William Street
PERTH, WA 6000
Phone: (08) 9321 9711 (after 5 May 1997)

NORTHERN TERRITORY

Relationships Australia
Northern Territory Inc
HEAD OFFICE
Ground Floor, Winlow House
75 Woods Street
DARWIN, NT 0800
Phone: (08) 8981 6676

TASMANIA

Anglicare Tasmania Inc
HEAD OFFICE
Level 1
29 Elizabeth Mall
HOBART TAS 7000
Phone: (03) 6223 4595

Centacare Family Services
HEAD OFFICE
23 Stoke Street
NEWTOWN, TAS 7008
Phone: (03) 6278 1660

Relationships Australia
Tasmania
HEAD OFFICE
306 Murray Street
HOBART, TAS 7000
Phone: (03) 6231 3141

ALL STATES

For Marriage Encounter and *Engaged Encounter*, contact your local church or the phone book in your nearest capital city.

NEW ZEALAND

Catholic Social Services
PO Box 4237
Christchurch
Phone: 0-3-379 0012

Presbyterian Support Services Executive Officer
Level 1
Laughton House
100 Tory Street
Wellington
Phone: 0-4-801 6005

Relationship Services
NATIONAL OFFICE
Ansett House
69–71 Boulcott Street
Wellington
Phone: 0-4-472 8798

UNITED KINGDOM

Relate National Marriage Guidance
Herbert Gray College
Little Church Street
Rugby
Warwickshire CV21 3AP
Phone: 0178 857 3241

Marriage Care
Clitherow House
1 Blythe Mews
Blythe Road
London
W14 0NW
Phone: *0171 371 1341*

Appendix B:
A renewal of marriage vows

This could be used either privately, with your immediate family, or in a larger church or other setting. It is not necessary to have an ordained person present, but it could be helpful at times. In the case of a couple wanting their civil marriage blessed, it would certainly be appropriate to contact the local church.

Some churches conduct an annual renewal of marriage service for the whole parish in which they may include special prayers for those who choose the single life, the divorced and those whose partners have died.

✠ A RITE OF RENEWAL OF MARRIAGE

You may care to read the Preface to the Marriage Service in your Prayer Book which recalls the purpose of marriage.

Following this, share these prayers and the renewal of vows together:

God our Father, in your great love for humankind you have given us the gift of marriage; so bless us both (and our children) as we renew the pledge of our lives and our love to each other, that our love may evermore grow to be the true reflection of your love for us, through Jesus Christ our Lord. Amen.

Take each other's right hand and renew your vows:
The man shall say to the woman:

I, [name], in the presence of God,
take you, [name], to be my wife;
to have and to hold
from this day forward,
for better, for worse,
for richer, for poorer,
in sickness and in health,
to love and to cherish,
so long as we both shall live.
This is my solemn vow.

The woman shall then say:

I, [name], in the presence of God,
take you, [name], to be my husband;
to have and to hold
from this day forward,
for better, for worse,
for richer, for poorer,
in sickness and in health,
to love and to cherish,
so long as we both shall live.
This is my solemn vow.

Acknowledging their wedding ring(s), the couple may then share these words:

[Name], I gave you this ring as a symbol of our marriage. With all that I am and all that I have I honour you; in the name of God. Amen.

To which the other may reply:

[Name], I received this ring from you as a symbol of your love and faithfulness to the end of our days.

You may like to share one or more of the following readings from the Bible:

Psalm 128
I Corinthians 13
John 2, verses 1 to 11
John 15, verses 9 to 16

Then say together:

All praise to you, God of love, creator of the universe, maker of man and woman in your likeness, source of blessing for married life.

All praise to you for you have created courtship and marriage, joy and gladness, feasting and laughter, pleasure and delight.

May your blessing come in full upon us.

May we know your presence in our joys and in our sorrows.

May we reach old age in the company of friends and come at last to your eternal kingdom. Amen.

and conclude with this prayer:

May God the Father lovingly enfold us,
God the Son grace our home and table,
God the Holy Spirit crown us with joy and peace.
May the Lord bless us and keep us in eternal life. Amen.

Suggestion: Now open some champagne, go out for dinner or do whatever the mood dictates![1]

Appendix C:
You and your funeral

The following pages are designed to help you plan your own funeral. By giving some consideration to the matter now, you will ensure that your wishes are observed, you will greatly assist the clergy and those responsible for your funeral, and you will make the arrangements easier for your family and loved ones.

You might wish to discuss these matters with your family, with clergy and with a funeral director. When you have talked it over, write out your list of directions, using this appendix as a guide. You should give the completed document to your clergyperson and a copy to your next of kin. The clergy will retain this in a confidential file. Perhaps give one to the funeral director and keep a copy yourself.

✠ The funeral service

A variety of combinations of services are available for the funeral. Please consider the following very carefully and then try to make some assessment of that combination which best suits you. There is no *right* way — what suits one person will not suit another. And customs are constantly changing, so you should not be greatly influenced simply by that.

You should try to choose a way which best expresses how you have lived (and worshipped). In an important way, your funeral is an attempt to express what you have believed:

* whether you wish to be buried or cremated
* whether you wish a public or a private service
* whether you want a church service or a service only at the graveside or crematorium. (A church service is recommended to practising believers, followed by either a private or public cremation or burial. Some churches have memorial gardens for ashes. You may like your service to include Holy Communion.)

✠ Funeral details

Your full name ______________________________

Your next of kin ____________________________

I would like my funeral to be organised in the following way:

____

____

____

____

If you have chosen a funeral director, please indicate:

____

____

I would like these hymns to be sung:

____

____

____

There are many suitable readings for funerals. Please consider the following (one reading from the Old Testament or New Testament and one from a Gospel would be appropriate):

Job 19: 1, 23–27b
1 Thessalonians 4: 13–18
Wisdom 3: 1–9c
2 Timothy 2: 8–13
Wisdom 4: 7–15
1 John 3: 1–2
Isaiah 25: 6–9
1 John 3: 14–16
Daniel 12: 1–3
Revelation 14: 13
Acts 10: 34–43
Matthew 11: 25–30
Romans 6: 3–9
Matthew 25: 31–46
Romans 8: 14–23
Mark 15: 33–39
Romans 8: 31b–35 and 37–39
Luke 12: 35–40
Romans 14: 7–9, 10b–12
Luke 23: 33, 39–43
1 Corinthians 15: 20–28
John 6: 37–40

2 Corinthians 5: 1 and 6–10
John 6: 51–58
2 Corinthians 15: 51–57
John 11: 17–27
Philippians 3: 20–21
John 12: 23–26
You might wish to choose a Psalm.
Consider these: 23, 25, 27, 42, 63, 103, 116, 122, 130, 143.

I would like the following readings:

____

____

It is recommended that you plan all the arrangements with the funeral director, too, including costs. Pre-paid funerals are a good idea and can be a saving, as well as giving peace of mind to your relatives at time of loss.

It would be a great help to the clergy or others preparing a eulogy to have a clear understanding of the details of your life. Not only does this ensure accuracy, but it makes sure that your story may be properly told. So it would be helpful to complete the following in full.

Remember, your requests will be kept in private files to be seen only by the clergy and those concerned at the time of your funeral.

Your full name ____________________________

Born ______________ Where __________________

Parents __________________________________

Education _______________________________

Early life ________________________________

Married __________________________________

When ________________

War service? ________________________________

Other ____________________________________

Children? ________________________________

____

Grandchildren (number) ________________________

Great-grandchildren (number) ____________________

Details of life and career, with dates if you wish:

____

____

____

____

Hobbies, sports and other interests:

____

____

Closest living relative ________________________

________________ phone ____________________

Closest living friend __________________________

________________ phone ____________________

Greatest interest(s) ____________________________

____

Dislikes __________________________________

Guiding principle of my life ____________________

Endnotes

Introduction

1. Robert Runcie, in *Church Times*, 6 July 1984
2. Jack Dominian, *Make or Break*, SPCK, 1984, p.57

Chapter 1

1. Howell Witt, *Witt's End*, Western Mount, 1981, p.5
2. The *West Australian*, 14 January 1991
3. Larry Crabb, *Inside Out*, Navpress, 1988, p.42
4. *An Australian Prayer Book*, Anglican Information Office, Sydney 1978, p.258
5. Edwin Muir, 'The Annunciation', *Collected Poems*, Faber and Faber, 1960, p.117

Chapter 2

1. Richard Holloway, *Seven to Flee, Seven to Follow*, Mowbray, 1986, p.28
2. Frances de Sales, *Introduction to the Devout Life*, Bk III. 9, in A. Squire Morehouse (ed.), *Asking the Fathers*, Barlow, 1973, p.190
3. John Smith, *Advance Australia Where?*, ANZEA, 1988, p.113
4. Jack Dominian, *An Introduction to Marital Problems*, Fount, 1986, pp.32–33
5. Howell Witt, *op. cit.*, pp.8–9

Chapter 3

1. *An Australian Prayer Book*, *op. cit.*, p.560
2. Keith Rayner, Mothers' Union World Conference, Brisbane, 1989

3. I am indebted to Louis Tice, *Investment in Excellence*, The Pacific Institute, Washington, 1980, for this definition of attitude.
4. John Smith, *op. cit.*, pp.108–109
5. Ephesians 4, verses 15 and 16
6. David Thornton-Wakeford, *If Fish Is All You Want*, Anglican Design, Display and Print, p.45

Chapter 4

1. Psalm 139, verses 13 to 16
2. L. Tice uses this description in *Investment in Excellence, op.cit.*
3. Brian Howard in *Sound of Living Waters*, Pulkingham and Harper (eds), Hodder & Stoughton, 1978
4. Psalm 139, verses 13 to 16

Chapter 5

1. John Powell, *The Secret of Staying in Love*, Argus, 1974, p.70
2. *Ibid*, p.76
3. *Ibid*, p.73
4. A. Craddock, *Becoming Married*, Prepare-Enrich, 1990, p.17
5. Matthew 7, verses 24 to 27
6. Richard Foster, *Celebration of Discipline*, Hodder & Stoughton, 1980 and *Freedom of Simplicity*, Harper & Row, 1981

Chapter 6

1. Augustine's commentary on John, in *Epist. Joann. Tractatus*, Romans vii, viii.
2. John 13, verses 34 and 35; chapter 15, verses 9 to 11
3. 1 Corinthians 13, verses 4 to 7
4. Thomas Merton, in James Forest, *Thomas Merton: A Pictorial Biography*, Paulist Press, 1980, p.59
5. Thomas Merton, *The Power and Meaning of Love*, Sheldon, 1976, p. 27
6. Gabrielle Bossis, *He and I*, Editiones Paulines, 1980, pp.110, 116 and 126
7. Romans 5, verses 1 to 5
8. Galatians 4, verses 4 to 6
9. Romans 8, verses 15 to 17
10. *An Australian Prayer Book*, Marriage Service, *op. cit.*, p.560 — italics mine.
11. *If Fish Is All You Want*, *op. cit.*, p.61
12. Ephesians 1, verses 3 to 10

13. John 10, verse 15
14. Galatians 6, verse 14
15. *An Australian Prayer Book, op. cit.*, p.561

Chapter 7

1. John 13, verses 37 and 38
2. Luke 22, verses 61 and 62
3. Prayer of Preparation, *An Australian Prayer Book, op. cit.*, p.135
4. Luke 15, verses 11 to 32
5. *An Australian Prayer Book, op. cit.*, p.173
6. See John 2, verse 25
7. 1 Corinthians 13, verse 5

Chapter 8

1. 2 Samuel 12, verses 13 and 14
2. 2 Samuel 12, verses 20 to 23
3. John 8, verses 3 to 11
4. Anglican General Synod Doctrine Commission, *A Christian Discussion on Sexuality: A Position Paper for General Synod*, 1989, pp.15–16
5. Luke 7, verses 36 to 50
6. Mark 10, verse 7; and John 8, verse 7
7. 1 Corinthians 7, verse 11; and 2 Corinthians 5, verse 17
8. Jack Dominian, Spirituality School, Wollaston College, Perth, August 1984. Dr Dominian is also the Founding Director of the Marriage Research Centre and the author of a number of books on the subject of marriage.
9. From the hymn, *Praise My Soul*, Psalm 103, Australian Hymn Book, Collins, 1976, No.68
10. David Thornton-Wakeford, *op. cit.*, p.47

Chapter 9

1. See 1 Kings 19, verse 12
2. *An Australian Prayer Book, op. cit.*, p.548
3. Og Mandino at the Celebrity Theatre, USA
4. Matthew 18, verse 3
5. David Thornton-Wakeford, *op. cit.*, p.11
6. Nadine Stair (an adaptation)

Chapter 10

1. Jack Dominian, *Introduction to Marriage Problems*, Fount, 1986, p.105

2. *An Australian Prayer Book, op. cit.*, p.561
3. 'Togetherness', Carmelite Monastery, Tallow, Co. Waterford
4. Matthew 22, verse 30

Postscript

1. John 14, verse 23

Appendix B

1. Adapted from *An Australian Prayer Book*, Service of Marriage 2nd Order, *op. cit.*, p.560ff and *A Prayer Book for Australia*, 1st and 2nd Orders of Marriage, The Anglican Church Trust Corporation, E.J. Dwyer, 1995, p.647ff.